The
Complete
LETTER
WRITER

THE
COMPLETE
LETTER WRITER

*How to write a letter for all
occasions, with numerous
specimen letters*

W. FOULSHAM & CO., LTD.

NEW YORK   TORONTO   CAPE TOWN   SYDNEY

W. FOULSHAM & CO. LTD
Bennetts Close, Cippenham, Berks, England

W. FOULSHAM & CO. LTD

ISBN 0-572-00002-2

Printed in Great Britain by
St Edmundsbury Press Ltd,
Bury St Edmunds, Suffolk

HOW TO USE THIS BOOK

We will suppose that you have a letter to write and that you do not feel equal to the task. It may be that letter writing is not in your line or, perhaps, the particular letter that is troubling you deals with details unfamiliar to you.

In any case, your first step is to run through this book and find if there is a specimen letter included which deals exactly with your subject. If there is, you can go ahead at once and follow the wording given, making whatever alterations are necessary regarding names, addresses, dates, and so on.

On the other hand, if there is no specimen which fits your case exactly, there is sure to be one that deals with a matter somewhat similar to yours. For instance, you may be wanting to write a letter to a person reminding him that he has not paid the rent of a garage which you lease him. There is no specimen devoted to this matter, but there are one or more letters referring to the overdue rent of houses. Though the things at issue are different, the way to write of them is the same. Therefore, you take one of the house letters, alter the parts that do not apply and there you have exactly what you want for garages.

It should not be overlooked that by using a passage from one specimen letter and piecing it into another letter, you may be able to say more satisfactorily what you fancy. When doing this, great care must be taken to see that the style of the two portions agree. For instance, one part must not say " I " and the other say " We."

In all cases, it is necessary to copy the arrangement and punctuation of the opening address, the date and the salutations, as any departure may make them incorrect.

From what has been said, it becomes clear that anyone who has a letter to write will find assistance in the specimens that are given, no matter what the letter is about.

CONTENTS

CONTENTS

Publishers' Note.—All the names and addresses in this book are purely fictitious. If any happen to be those of real people or places, it is mere coincidence.

The
Complete Letter Writer

I

HOW TO WRITE A LETTER

Someone has said that " the letter you write is you."
If this is so, it is very certain that every letter we send
out should be our best work, in order that the recipient
may get a good impression of us.

A good letter calls for many qualities. Not only
should the matter be well phrased and written, or typed,
but the paper should be of suitable quality, the envelope
properly addressed and spaced, the stamp stuck on in
its allotted area, and so on.

Let us take these matters and consider them in detail.
First, the notepaper. This should be of good quality,
plain with nothing fanciful ; therefore, no deckled edges
or coloured borders. Sheet of quarto size are handy
to read and better than folded notepaper for all but
personal or intimate correspondence. The paper and
the envelope should match, except when an envelope
with an embossed stamp (purchased from a post office)
is used, or when several sheets are enclosed in a large
envelope.

Should you be using folded notepaper, start your
letter on page 1. If what you wish to write will occupy
two pages, continue and finish on page 4. Should you
consider three or four pages necessary, use them in order
namely, 1, 2, 3, 4, finishing on either pages 3 or 4.

Commence with your own address in full and, then, give the date. Both these should be placed close to the upper right-hand corner.

On a level with the date, but on the left of the paper, write the name of the person who is to receive the letter, if it is a business communication and, on the next line, follow with the salutation, " Dear Sir," " Dear Madam," " Sir," " Madam," or whatever is appropriate. If, however, it is a friendly letter, start with " Dear Joan," " Dear Miss Smith," " Dear Fred," or whatever is correct in the circumstances.

Then, having set out the preliminaries, start with the actual letter. In piecing together the body, a number of rules must be observed. Probably, the opening sentence will be the hardest to frame, because once you have managed to make a beginning, the subsequent passages will follow naturally on to those gone before. If you cannot think of a suitable beginning, glance through the specimen letters in this book. There is obviously a beginning to each and there ought to be dozens that will suit your purpose.

But, whatever you do, do not be tempted to start off with a phrase beloved by some ignorant writers, " I trust you are well, as this leaves me at present." The phrase is hackneyed, it is ungrammatical, it does not mean what it says and it is bad in every way.

It is much better to say nothing about your health until reaching the end of the letter, and, then, only in a friendly letter. A good way to speak of it is to say something like this : " All of us at home are enjoying good health and we trust that it is the same with you."

Business letters are often commenced with the formula, " I beg to acknowledge the receipt of your letter of so and so, and to state in reply . . ." Many authorities deprecate this form of opening, but there is no doubt that it is straightforward and to the point : it also links up in the mind of the recipient some former communication.

Having plunged into the letter, get to the real facts at once. Say what you have to say clearly and briefly and do not use involved sentences which admit of two or more meanings.

Do not be tempted to use the third person in expressing yourself, unless you are dealing with a formal invitation, and, of course, you must not mix up the first and third person in the same document. Some time ago, we came across a letter in which this mixing of persons was beautifully illustrated. The letter began with, " Dear Sir, Mrs. Brown presents her compliments and I would like to know why the goods have not yet arrived."

After brevity, the next consideration is courtesy. Avoid a haughty manner, but this does not mean that you should go to the other extreme and become servile. If you have anything unpleasant to say, think twice or even thrice before you say it. Personally, we have written many letters with a sting in them, but our invariable plan is never to post such an epistle until twenty-four hours after it has been penned. The act of writing the caustic letter seems to serve the purpose of a safety-valve and, once the steam has blown off, we feel more composed about the matter, and the letter ends by being consigned to the fire. Our advice then is this : Do not write an abusive letter but, if you must, then write it and sleep on it. After that, you will probably prefer to burn rather than send it.

Let your remarks be framed in a composed style, not in the breathless haste which suggests a whirlwind. We all know the kind of person who tells us that he or she is in a " terrific hurry " or is " dreadfully busy." What we are really being told is that he or she begrudges the time that is being wasted on writing to us. And, next to the whirlwind type of letter is the gushing letter in which things are " fearfully beautiful " and everybody is a darling. Such remarks are tiresome.

Never commit yourself to libellous statements in a

letter. In the first case, it is uncharitable and, in the second, it may draw you into all sorts of unpleasant situations. As with libellous remarks, so with gossipy scandal. Avoid it at all costs, since you never know into whose hands your communication may fall.

Certain hackneyed phrases are best avoided. People write, " Yours to hand and thanking you for *same*." The word " same," used in this way, stamps the writer as a person with a poor mastery of words. The word " favour," meaning a " letter," is also weak. " Re," at the head of a letter, can help to save time in tracing matters, but " re " in the body of a letter is usually poor, e.g.. " I saw Mr. Jones, yesterday, re what we were discussing." Latin abbreviations such as " ult.", " inst." and " prox." should be used sparingly. Far better give the actual name of the month.

Invariably indicate the date on your letter ; see to it that the recipient's name and initials are given correctly ; read the letter over before sealing it ; check the facts and figures, if any, and be sure, if enclosures are mentioned, that they really are enclosed. Finally, make certain that you put the letter in the right envelope.

Business Letters

Letters sent out by business houses should be typed on one side only of good quality paper. If the paper has no printed letter heading, the address of the sender should appear at the top in full. A little lower down on the left-hand side of the paper, the name of the recipient should appear. The salutation—" Dear Sir," " Dear Madam," " Sir " or " Madam "—as the case may be should follow, and under this, if possible, a heading underlined, as " re Your Outstanding Account." The subject matter follows. This should be concise, but not laconic. Decide what you want to say, and say it in the fewest possible words consistent with politeness. The sentences should not be too long, and the whole matter should be broken up into reasonably short paragraphs.

When single-space typing is used for the body of the letter, two lines should be left between the paragraphs. If the letter is short, double spacing looks better, but use single spacing for a long one. About five spaces " indentation " should be left on the left-hand side of the paper when starting a fresh paragraph, and letters always look better if a fairly wide margin (say about fifteen spaces on the typewriter) be left.

Do not be florid or servile. Do not drop into the lazy habit of using the stereotyped jargon so common in big houses ; the tiresome habit of stereotyped phrases is easily acquired, and hard to discard. Pay your clients the compliment of writing a different letter to each, even though writing about the same subject matter to all. Conclude a business letter with " Yours faithfully," or " Yours truly."

If there is any enclosure, it is a good plan to inscribe " Enclosure " in the bottom left-hand corner of the sheet, as a guide to the postal clerk. Don't sign with the typewriter or with a stamp—it does not take long to sign your name. If the signature is illegible, it is a good plan to type the name (in brackets) under the signature.

Fold the letter neatly and evenly in two or three folds, according to the size of the envelope. The cover should be addressed exactly in accordance with the subscription inside the letter. If a " window envelope " is used, the letter should be folded with the writing outside, and placed in the envelope with the address showing through the transparency. See that all enclosures are in the envelope before sealing up. It should not be necessary to stress the necessity of stamping letters properly, but the experience of the Post Office is that an amazingly large number of packages are placed in the letter boxes without prepaying the postage.

How to Begin a Letter

(1) *Dear Sir,*
(2) *Dear Madam,*
Either of the above is usual in all business correspondence.
(3) *Sir,*
(4) *Madam,*
These are equally appropriate, but a trifle more severe than the previous.
(5) *Dear Sirs,*
This is the correct opening when the letter is addressed to " Messrs. So and So." As an alternative, " Sirs," can be used.
(6) *Gentlemen,*
Sometimes used instead of (5), but is now largely out of fashion.
Note that if any of the above are written, the person's name must precede them.

(7) *Dear Mr. Jones,*
(8) *Dear Mrs. Brown,*
(9) *Dear Miss Smith,*
All the above are correct when the writer is personally acquainted with the person receiving the letter.

(10) *Dear Miss,*
This is never correct and should never be written.

(11) *Dear Tom or My Dear Tom,*
(12) *Dear Alice or My Dear Alice,*
To be used when the friendship between writer and receiver is close.

(13) *My Darling Tom, My Dearest Mary,*
are correct for special cases of affection.

Phrases for Beginning Letters

If you are hesitating for a phrase with which to commence your letter, probably one of the following will suit your purpose :

I am very much obliged to you—
In reply to your letter of—
It was very good of you to—
I am sorry to have to say that—
It is so long since you wrote that—
I am wondering if you could—
In accordance with your request—
Please accept my thanks for—
Enclosed please find—
Would you be good enough to—
Many thanks for your letter of
I regret to inform you that—
I must thank you for—
Could you favour me with—
I greatly appreciate your—
In acknowledging your letter of—
Referring to your letter of—
We hasten to thank you for—
I am anxious to hear from you about—
You will, no doubt, be interested to hear—
We wish to remind you that—
I have to point out that—
Your letter gave me—
We submit, herewith,—
I have carefully considered your—
Recently, we had occasion to write to you about—
I am pleased to confirm your letter of—
With reference to your letter of—
It is with considerable pleasure (regret) that I —
Many thanks for the beautiful—
You will be sorry, I know, to hear that—
I find it necessary to—

How to Close a Letter

(1) *Yours faithfully,*

A safe ending for all business letters.

(2) *Yours truly,* and *Yours very truly,*

Correct for business letters, when something a little more friendly than (1) is required.

(3) *Yours sincerely,*

A safe ending for all personal letters.

(4) *Yours affectionately,*

Suitable for relations, would-be relations and between girl friends, but now usually replaced by (3).

(5) *Yours cordially,*

Used by rather old-fashioned people who wish to write something not so ordinary as (3).

(6) *Faithfully yours,* and (2) to (5)

can be given the reverse order of the words. It is a matter of taste.

(7) *Yours respectfully,*

Not advised as it is too servile.

(8) *Your obedient servant,*

Only to be used in certain official letters.

(9) *Yours ever,*

Only to be used when writing to a close friend.

The Address on the Notepaper

(1) Do not give the name of a house in inverted commas. Thus, write *Pembridge*, not " *Pembridge.*"

(2) Formerly it was correct to follow the number of the house by a comma. It is still correct to do so, but most people omit it.

(3) The words " road ", " street ", " avenue ", etc., may be written with a capital or small letter. Either is correct, but a capital is, perhaps, the better. If they end the line, follow them with a comma.

(4) The words " road ", " street ", etc., may be shortened, if desired, to " rd." " st.", etc. If they are so

THE SPACING OF A TYPED LETTER

Note how the various spaces are flush at the sides and that the whole effect is one of balance. In the case of a handwritten letter, there should be an attempt to gain the same balanced effect.

shortened, a full stop must follow. And, if they end the line, there must be a comma following the full stop.

(5) At the end of all lines in the address, a comma is needed, except in the case of the last line, when a full stop is required.

The Date

Every letter should be dated.

The date should come after the address, on the right-hand side of the sheet.

There are many ways in which it can be given correctly. Thus :

(1) January 1, 19—.

(2) January 2nd, 19—.

(3) Jan. 3, 19—. (Full stop after Jan.)

(4) 4 January, 19—.

(5) 5 Jan., 19—. (Full stop and comma after Jan.)

(6) Jan. 6th, 19—. (Full stop after Jan.)

(7) 7 : 1 : 37.

(8) 8—1—37.

Forms (7) and (8) should be generally avoided.

Addressing an Envelope

The address on an envelope gives the recipient his first impression of what is likely to be within. If it is well executed, the impression will be a good one, but if the wording is badly arranged, it will certainly be unfavourable.

To space the wording properly, imagine a line cutting the envelope into two equal spaces, one above the other : then if you write a normal size and the address is of ordinary length, start writing the name slightly below this imaginary line. If, however, your handwriting is large and the address is somewhat lengthy, begin on the imaginary line, or even a little higher. Of course, you will not start actually on the left-hand edge, but slightly inwards.

The name being written, you will set out the address
in two, three or more lines, whichever is necessary.
Each line will be indented a little more than the one
above, or, if you prefer to adopt the newer method, you
will begin each fresh line absolutely flush with the line
above.

Of course, you will affix the stamp in the upper right-
hand corner, and it should be put straight.   To tilt it or
place it upside down is a breach of etiquette.

Here are some specimens worth noting ı

(1)　　　　　　B. A. Williams Esq.,
　　　　　　　　Hatcherley,
　　　　　　　　　Lane End,
　　　　　　　　　　Brighton.

(2)　　　　　James Phillips Esq., M.P.
　　　　　　　　House of Commons,
　　　　　　　　　London, S.W.1.

(3)　　　　　Mr. Bertram Davidson,
　　　　　　　　38, Victoria Rd.,
　　　　　　　　　Westbridge,
　　　　　　　　　　Surrey.

(4)　　　　　Mrs. Bertram Davidson,
　　　　　　　　38, Victoria Road,
　　　　　　　　　Westbridge,
　　　　　　　　　　Surrey.

(5)　　　　　Miss Alice Turnbull,
　　　　　　　　51, Cadogan Row,
　　　　　　　　　Wigan,
　　　　　　　　　　Lancs.

(6)　　　　　Messrs. Warren & Bourne.
　　　　　　　　Timber Merchants,
　　　　　　　　　3, Green Road,
　　　　　　　　　　West Bridgford,
　　　　　　　　　　　Nottinghamshire.

(7)　　　　The Thames Timber Co., Ltd.,
　　　　　　　54, Wharf Lane,
　　　　　　　　　London, E.C.1.

(8)   <u>Please forward</u>
                    Mrs. Eagles,
                          16, Derrymore Street,
                          Pimlico,
                                London, S.W.1
(9)   The Managing Director,
                    The Thames Timber Co., Ltd.,
                    54, Wharf Lane,
                    London, E.C.1.

Now to consider these nine specimens, No. 1 uses the
title " Esq." and not " Mr." The former is in better
style than the latter. Note that it is fussy to write
" Esqre," and wrong to put " Esquire." Also note that
" Mr. B. A. Williams Esq." is a bad mistake.

No. 2 shows that abbreviated titles come after the
designation, " Esq." Thus, " James Phillips, M.P.,
Esq." is wrong.

No. 3 gives " Mr." as the designation, though, as we
have said above, it is not so good as " Esq." If " Mr."
is written, it should be followed by a full stop, as it is an
abbreviation.

No. 4 shows that in addressing a married lady, it is
correct to give her husband's Christian name. It is
wrong to write " Mrs. Mary Davidson." Note, also,
that being an abbreviation, " Mrs." must be followed
by a full stop. In the case of the word " Road," in
No. 3, it is shortened to " Rd.," therefore it requires a
full stop because it is abbreviated and a comma, because
it is the end of a section of the address. In No. 4, however, " Road " is given in full and thus only needs the
comma.

No. 5.—In this case, " Miss " commences the address.
No full stop follows the word, as it does with " Mr."
and " Mrs.", because " Miss " is not an abbreviated word.

Nos. 6 and 7 show that " Messrs." should only be
employed in the form of address to a firm whose name

incorporates that of an individual. This rule applies to the commencement of a business letter, as well as to the envelope.

No. 8 is a request that the letter should be redirected to an address unknown by the writer.

No. 9 shows the flush starting form of address which is becoming a favourite method with typists, as it saves a slight amount of time.

The Postmaster-General requests writers to observe the following rules, as the time of postmen and sorters is, thereby, saved :

1. Use the number of the house, if it has one, and not just the name of the house.

2. In the case of flats, chambers and suites of offices, the number of the flat, etc., and its floor or block should be included.

3. The area post code must always be included.

4. In country districts, the nearest post town should be given in addition to the actual village, hamlet, etc.

5. Do not use the name of the county town, when the name of the county is intended. Thus do not write " Cambridge " when " Cambridgeshire " is correct.

6. Do not write " Local," but use the name of the post town.

The Use of Postcards

Postcards provide a handy, quick and cheap way of sending messages. Their use, however, should not be abused, as so often happens. Whenever we see a card closely packed with small writing, we may be almost certain that the sender has overlooked the real mission of the postcard. Its use, as we say, is to send a hurried note; but the note should be quite impersonal. There should be nothing of a private or intimate nature about what is written. If the message goes beyond this, it is in bad taste. The writer may be somewhat thick-skinned and not mind how much of his—it is usually " her "—

affairs are broadcast, but he should think of the receiver who, probably, does mind.

Therefore, it is well to remember that if you expose private business on a postcard, your friends will hardly thank you.

Writing to Persons of Title

THE QUEEN.—Her Most Gracious Majesty Queen Elizabeth II. *Commence :* Madam, *or* May it please your Majesty. *Conclude :* I have the honour to remain, your Majesty's most faithful servant.

ROYAL PRINCES.—His Royal Highness (then give title). *Commence :* Sir. *Conclude :* I have the honour to remain, Sir, Your Royal Highness's most dutiful servant.

ROYAL PRINCESSES.—Her Royal Highness (then give title). *Commence :* Madam. *Conclude :* I have the honour to remain, Madam, Your Royal Highness's most dutiful servant.

OTHER PRINCES AND PRINCESSES.—As above, but omit " Royal " and " most."

DUKE.—His Grace the Duke of ——. *Commence :* My Lord Duke. *Conclude :* I remain, my Lord Duke, Your Grace's most obedient servant.

DUCHESS.—Her Grace the Duchess of ——. *Commence:* Madam. *Conclude :* I remain, Madam, Your Grace's most obedient servant.

MARQUESS.—The Most Honourable, the Marquess of ——. *Commence :* My Lord Marquess. *Conclude :* I remain, my Lord Marquess, Your Lordship's most obedient servant.

MARCHIONESS.—The Most Honourable, the Marchioness of ——. *Commence :* Madam. *Conclude :* I remain, Madam, Your Ladyship's most obedient servant.

EARL.—The Right Honourable the Earl of ——.

Commence : My Lord. *Conclude :* I remain, my Lord, Your Lordship's most obedient servant.

COUNTESS.—The Right Honourable the Countess of ——. *Commence* and *Conclude* as for a Marchioness.

VISCOUNT.—The Right Honourable the Lord Viscount ——. *Commence* and *Conclude* as for an Earl.

VISCOUNTESS.—The Right Honourable the Lady Viscountess ——. *Commence* and *Conclude* as for a Marchioness.

BARON.—The Right Honourable Lord ——. *Commence* and *Conclude* as for an Earl.

BARONESS.—The Right Honourable Lady ——. *Commence* and *Conclude* as for a Marchioness.

BARONET.—Sir (Christian and Surname), Bt. (not Bart.). *Commence :* Sir. No special formula for concluding.

BARONET'S WIFE.—Lady (Surname only, unless born with a title). *Commence :* Madam. *Conclude :* As above.

ARCHBISHOP.—His Grace the Lord Archbishop of ——. *Commence :* My Lord Archbishop. *Conclude :* I remain, my Lord Archbishop, Your Grace's most obedient servant.

BISHOP.—The Right Rev. the Lord Bishop of ——. *Commence :* My Lord Bishop. *Conclude :* I remain, my Lord Bishop, Your Lordship's most obedient servant.

DEAN.—The Very Rev. the Dean of ——. *Commence :* Mr. Dean, *or* Very Reverend Sir. *Conclude :* I remain, Reverend Sir, Your most obedient servant.

ARCHDEACON.—The Venerable the Archdeacon ——. *Commence :* Mr. Archdeacon, *or* Reverend Sir. *Conclude* as for a Dean.

AMBASSADOR.—His Excellency H.B.M.'s Ambassador and Plenipotentiary to the Court of ——. *Commence* and *Conclude* according to rank.

AMBASSADOR'S WIFE.—According to rank.

GOVERNOR GENERAL.—His Excellency ——, Governor General of —— ; *or*, if a Duke, His Grace the Governor General of ——. *Commence* and *Conclude* according to rank.

GOVERNOR OF COLONY.—His Excellency ——, Governor

of ——. *Commence* and *Conclude* according to rank.

BRITISH CONSUL.—A. B. Esq., H.B.M.'s Agent and Consul (*or* Vice Consul, *or* Consul General, as case may be). No special formula for commencing or concluding.

PRIME MINISTER.—According to rank.

PRIVY COUNCILLOR.—To the Right Hon. —— *Commence* and *Conclude* according to rank.

SECRETARY OF STATE.—Her Majesty's Principal Secretary of State for the —— Department. *Commence* and *Conclude* according to rank.

LORD MAYOR.—To the Right Hon. The Lord Mayor of ——. *Commence :* My Lord. *Conclude :* Your Lordship's Obedient Servant.

MAYOR (OF A CITY OR OF HASTINGS, RYE, HYTHE, NEW ROMNEY). – The Right Worshipful the Mayor of —— (OF A TOWN) The Worshipful the Mayor of – *Commence:* Sir. *Conclude:* I remain, Sir, Your obedient servant.

ALDERMAN.—To Mr. Alderman A.B. *Commence :* Sir. No special formula for concluding. But in the case of a lady, the superscription is usually reversed, thus : To Alderman Miss A.B.

COUNCILLOR.—As for " Alderman " with the word " Councillor " substituted.

JUDGE (ENGLAND AND N. IRELAND).—The Hon. Sir A. B. (if a Knight) *or* The Hon. Mr. Justice A. B. *Commence :* Sir. *Conclude :* I have the honour to be, Sir, Your most obedient servant.

COUNTY COURT JUDGE.—To His Honour, Judge ——. *Commence* and *Conclude* as above.

SCOTTISH JUDGE (LORD OF SESSION).—The Hon. Lord ——. *Commence :* My Lord. *Conclude :* I have the honour to be, Your Lordship's most obedient servant.

KNIGHT.—Sir A.B. *Commence :* Sir. No special formula for concluding.

KNIGHT'S WIFE.—As for a Baronet's Wife.

MEMBER OF PARLIAMENT.—As in private life, with the addition of the letters M.P. after the name. If an esquire, place M.P. after Esq.

II

INVITATIONS AND THEIR REPLIES

All sorts of Invitations are dealt with in this section. The necessary replies—whether acceptances or refusals— are also given.

An Invitation to Dinner (Quite Informal)

> Ridgway House,
> Ridgway Lane,
> Reigate.
> Feb. 5th, 19—.

My dear Susan,

Will you be a dear and come along, with John, to dinner here on Thursday next, Feb. 10th ? It would be just right if you arrived about 6.30 p.m.

There will be a few friends here, but you have met them all before.

After dinner, if there is time, we hope to get in a few hands of Bridge.

Now, do write back and say that John and you can both manage it. We have not seen you for ages.

> With love,
> Marjorie.

Letter Accepting an Invitation to Dinner (Quite Informal)

> Northcote,
> Charlwood Drive,
> Reigate.
> Feb. 6th, 19—.

My dear Marjorie,

How nice of you to ask us both to come to dinner on Feb. 10th.

John and I will be delighted to accept your invitation. Need I say we are looking forward to a very jolly evening ?

John sends his love.

With love,
Susan.

(*Note that the letter repeats the date, so that if, by any chance, a mistake has been made, the fact will be brought to light and corrected.*)

Letter Refusing an Invitation to Dinner (Quite Informal)

Northcote,
Charlwood Drive,
Reigate.
Feb. 6th, 19—.

My dear Marjorie,

I am angry. Only yesterday, John accepted an invitation for us both to go over to friends at ——, on Thursday next. We cannot get out of it anyhow now ; so we have nothing else to do but to refuse you as nicely as we know how. Why did you not write a day or two earlier ?

You know we would have both loved to come.

With love,
Susan.

An Invitation to Dinner (Semi-Formal)

Ridgway House,
Ridgway Lane,
Reigate.
Feb. 5th, 19—.

Dear Mrs. Lovelace,

Will you and Mr. Lovelace give us the pleasure of your company at dinner on Thursday next, Feb. 10th (6.30 p.m.)?

We are asking a few friends, all of whom you have

met here previously.   Afterwards, we expect to find some time for Bridge.

It will be very nice if you can come, and we very much hope that you will.

> Yours sincerely,
> Marjorie Summers.

A Letter Accepting an Invitation

> Northcote,
> Charlwood Drive,
> Reigate.
> Feb. 6th, 19—.

Dear Mrs. Summers,

Very many thanks for your kind invitation.   My husband and I will be delighted to accept your invitation to dinner on Feb. 10th.

I need hardly tell you that we are both looking forward to seeing you.

> Yours sincerely,
> Letitia Lovelace.

(Note that a wife can speak or write of her husband in three ways.   She can use his Christian name ; . she can refer to him as " my husband ", or she can speak of him as " Mr. So-and-so."   If he is well known to the person receiving the letter, then the Christian name is suitable. " My husband " is safe in any circumstances.   The form " Mr. So-and-so " is now used only in conversation with servants, and should therefore not be used in social correspondence.

A Letter Refusing an Invitation (Semi-Formal)

> Northcote,
> Charlwood Drive,
> Reigate.
> Feb. 6th, 19—.

Dear Mrs. Summers,

Very many thanks for your kind invitation.

Unfortunately, my husband is in bed with a severe chill and the doctor will not allow him to get up for a day or two, so we shall not be able to be with you on Thursday. We are both very sorry.   Very many thanks.

Yours sincerely,
Letitia Lovelace.

Formal Invitation to Dinner

Mr. and Mrs. Arthur Mackie
Request the Pleasure of
* Mr. and Mrs. James Burchell's
Company
at Dinner on
Thursday, Sep. 28th, at 7.30 p.m.

30, Fortune's Row,
    Hartley.

(Naturally such an invitation is only sent when the occasion is very formal. The card should be printed, the starred line being filled in by hand.)

Reply to a Formal Invitation to Dinner

Mr. and Mrs. James Burchell have much pleasure in accepting Mr. and Mrs. Arthur Mackie's kind invitation to dinner on Thursday, Sep. 28th.

45, Fortune's Row,
    Hartley.   Sep. 20th, 19—.

OR

Mr. and Mrs. James Burchell much regret that owing to a prior engagement they are unable to accept Mr. and Mrs. Arthur Mackie's kind invitation to dinner on Thursday, Sep. 28th.

45, Fortune's Row,
    Hartley.   Sep. 20th, 19—.

Formal Invitation to a Wedding, suitable for being printed

Dr. and Mrs. Mervyn Giles
Request the pleasure of
* MISS BERYL THOMPSON'S
Company at the Marriage of their Daughter,
SUSAN,
to
Mr. Archer Jones,
at Holy Trinity Church, Mexford,
on Saturday, April 3rd, 19—,
at 2 o'clock
and afterwards at
Gunter's Hall, Mexford.

R.S.V.P.
The Hall, Mexford.

(The starred line is the only one that varies between one invitation and another.)

Reply to a Formal Invitation to a Wedding

The Red Roofs,
Mexford.

March 20th, 19—.

Miss Beryl Thompson thanks Dr. and Mrs. Mervyn Giles for their kind invitation to be present at the wedding of their daughter, Susan, to Mr. Archer Jones, which she has much pleasure in accepting.

OR

Miss Beryl Thompson has much pleasure in accepting the kind invitation of Dr. and Mrs. Mervyn Giles to be present at the wedding of their daughter, Susan, to Mr. Archer Jones.

Formal Invitation to a Dance

Mr. and Mrs. A. E. Clarke
request the pleasure of
* Mr. and Mrs. Stoneham's
Company on
Saturday, December 4th, 19—.

The Horns,   Dancing 9.30—2.30
  Chertsey Vale.   R.S.V.P.

OR

Mrs. A. E. Clarke
requests the pleasure of
* Miss Ruby Water's
Company on
Thursday, January 8th, 19—.

The Horns,   Dancing 8.30—1 a.m.
  Chertsey Vale.   R.S.V.P.

(The starred line is varied in the case of each guest who is invited. The reply should be in the third person to match the above. Usually such an invitation as this is printed.)

Formal Reply to a Formal Invitation to a Dance

Mr. and Mrs. Stoneham
Have Great Pleasure in Accepting
Mr. and Mrs. A. E. Clarke's
Invitation for Saturday, Dec. 4th.

The Kennels,
  Chertsey Vale.

OR

Miss Ruby Waters
Thanks Mrs. A. E. Clarke
for her kind invitation
for Thursday, January 8th,
and Very Much Regrets that
she is unable to accept it.

The Pantiles,
  Chertsey Vale.

Reply to the Previous Invitation

> The Hollyhocks,
>> Chertsey Vale.
>>> Nov. 26th, 19—.

Mr. and Mrs. Stoneham wish to thank Mr. and Mrs. A. E. Clarke for their kind invitation for Dec. 4th, and have much pleasure in accepting.

OR

. . . and much regret that a prior engagement prevents them from accepting.

Letter of Invitation for a Musical Evening

> The Poplars,
>> Northcote Lane,
>>> Twickenham.
>>>> Nov. 3rd, 19—.

Dear Miss Allison,

We are having a few friends with us on Friday, Nov 8th, and should be delighted if you could form one of our number.

We intend to have some music, so will you bring your songs? Do come, and please try to be here about 7.30 p.m.

> Yours sincerely,
>> Mary Robson.

An " At-Home " Invitation

* Mrs. Jeeves,
Mrs. Arthur Prince
At Home
Four to Six-thirty—Thursday,
Dec. 18th.

Ferndale,
  Snake's Lane,
    Burton.

(An " at-home " invitation is sent out on an engraved printed card, the wording being as above. The starred

name is written on the card and it is that of the person invited. Thus, in this case, Mrs. Jeeves is invited by Mrs. Prince.

No acceptance or refusal is needed. Friends merely " drop in.")

Letter of Invitation to a Twenty-first Birthday Party

61, Tregunter Park,
Fulham, S.W.6.

March 20th, 19—.

Captain and Mrs. Arthur Brown
Request the Pleasure of
* Miss Alice Mackenzie
at an Evening Party
to be held on April 2nd, at 8.45 p.m.
at the above address to
Celebrate the Coming of Age
of their daughter
Vivienne.

R.S.V.P.

(As a rule, the above is printed, with the starred line filled in by hand. Close friends are sent a card, as above, with a personal note scribbled in one corner. The reply is worded on the lines of the specimen given for a dance.)

Letter of Invitation to a Children's Party

17, Burnside Avenue,
South Ham,
Essex.

Dec. 19th, 19—.

Dear Mrs. Alston,

Marion and David are having a few of their friends to a party here, on Tuesday, January 3rd, and they are hoping that John will be able to come. It is between 4.30 and 9 p.m.

If you are thinking of coming to fetch him, it would be so nice if you arrived about 7 p.m. Then, you would be in time for some of the fun.

Do try to manage this, as I shall be so pleased to see you.

Yours sincerely,

Mary Seymour.

(This letter is, of course, written by the mother of Marion and David.)

Letter Accepting an Invitation to a Children's Party

24, Burnside Avenue,
South Ham,
Essex.

Dec. 22nd, 19—

Dear Mrs. Seymour,

John says " thank you very much " for the invitation to Marion and David's party. He is excited about it and hopes to come.

I will drop in about 7 p.m., as you suggest, just to have a chat.

Looking forward to seeing you,

Yours sincerely,

Marjorie Alston.

(Note the possessive case in the above. Both Marion and David are concerned equally, but the rule is that when two names are used to infer possession, only the second one is given the apostrophe s.)

Letter Refusing an Invitation to a Children's Party

24, Burnside Avenue,
South Ham,
Essex.

Dec. 22nd, 19—.

Dear Mrs. Seymour,

John is most upset that he will not be able to

accept the invitation for the party on January 3rd.

We always spend Christmas with my husband's people down in Devonshire, and we shall be away a fortnight.

Will you please thank Marion and David and tell them how sorry John is that he will not be able to come ?

It was extremely nice of you to ask him.

> Yours sincerely,
>> Marjorie Alston.

Letter of Invitation to a Children's Party
(Quite Informal)

> 17, Burnside Avenue,
>> South Ham,
>>> Essex.
>>>> Dec. 19th, 19—.

Dear John,

We are hoping to have such a lovely party on Tuesday, January 3rd, and we want you to come, as it would not be complete without you.

Write and say " yes," please.

> Yours with love,
>> From
>>> Marion and David.

4.30 to 9 p.m.

(This is a suitable wording for either Marion or David to use, when they are attending to the invitations.)

Letter of Invitation to a Children's Party

> Thornleigh,
>> Wharfsdale.
>>> Jan. 10th, 19—.

Dear Mrs. Jones,

It is Dolly's birthday on Tuesday, the 17th, and my children are having a little party. We shall be so pleased if you will allow Kate and Alice to join them. Can you send them by 3.30 ? We like to be early as the children and their friends are all young—perhaps you could send for them at 8 o'clock.

With kindest regards,
Very sincerely yours,
Martha Dawkins.

Letter Inviting Children to a Party

369, Crescent Rd.,
Burton-on-Wash,
Norfolk.

Jan. 8th, 19—.

Dear Mrs. Henderson,

My children are getting up a little party for Tuesday, 15th January, to begin at about half-past seven, and we shall be so glad if you and your young people will give us the pleasure of your presence for the evening.

Yours very sincerely,
Laura Stevenson.

Letter of Invitation to a Children's Party

17, Burnside Avenue,
South Ham,
Essex.

Marion and David Seymour
Are Having a Party
for their friends
on Tuesday, January 3rd.
They Sincerely Hope that
* Master John Alston
will be good enough to accept
this invitation
to be present.

R.S.V.P.
4.30 to 9 p.m.

(The starred line is the only portion of the invitation

which needs altering for the various guests. Note that many children fancy this formal wording, as it gives the invitation an important appearance.)

Letter of Invitation to a Picnic

> The Kennels,
> Chertsey Vale.
> July 8th, 19—.

Dear Mr. Morris,

We propose to have a picnic at the Thicket on Friday, July 15th (weather permitting). We start from here at 12 noon. It would give us great pleasure if you could join us. May we hope to see you ?

If it rains we intend to have a few hands of Bridge instead.

> Yours sincerely,
> Joyce Jarman.

Letter Refusing the Previous

> The Ridges,
> Chertsey Vale.
> July 10th, 19—.

Dear Mrs. Jarman,

Your invitation to the picnic is tantalizing me, because I simply cannot come. On that afternoon, I am due to be far away in Devonshire, toiling for my bread and butter.

How I would have enjoyed being with you all, trying to make myself useful by pouring hot tea accidentally down ladies' necks ! It would have been great ; but it is not to be.

Please let me thank you for inviting me, and with every expression of regret,

> Yours sincerely,
> Arthur Morris.

Letter Inviting a Girl Friend to take Part in a Motor Tour

The Grey Towers,
Littlebourne,
Kent.

July 1st, 19—

Dear Peggy,

Will you come and join us in a motor tour ?   George is frightfully proud of a new car he has just bought and we want to have a really jolly tour through Wales.   If you can come—and we are tremendously set on your joining us—there will be you, and George and myself, and my brother Frank.   I think you have met Frank—anyway, he is quite sure he remembers you—so we ought to make a nice little party.   We thought of starting from here about the first of next month.   George thinks of mapping out the tour beforehand ; but of course it can be changed if anybody has any suggestions to make—but he will find out beforehand where are the best hotels and stopping-places.   Will you say which day you can come ?   Let it be a few days before we start, so that we can settle things and get off comfortably.

Yours with love,
Phyllis.

Letter Replying to an Invitation to take Part in a Motor Tour

Middle Cloisters,
Canterbury.

July 3rd, 19—

Dear Phyllis,

How jolly !   And how good of you to ask me to join you !   I shall love it above all things !   But do tell George to manage to get the Clerk of the Weather in a good temper !   Tell me what clothes I shall want, and about how long you propose to be on tour.

I should love to see Caernarvon and Bettws-y-Coed ; but there are so many lovely places in Wales that I shall be quite happy to fit in with your plans.   I suppose you will go to Tintern and Chepstow and Raglan.   If I come to you on the 28th, will that suit you ?

Yours, quite jumpy with joy,
Peggy.

Letter of Thanks after the Motor Tour

Middle Cloisters,
Canterbury.
July 29th, 19—.

Dear Phyllis,

Now that our lovely motor tour has come to an end and I am back at home, I want to thank you and George for a really delightful time.   I enjoyed every moment of it, and I think the way George planned it all was splendid. He seems to anticipate just what we girls want.

I found everybody and everything at home going on as usual.   Mother and Dad are getting tired of my stories about the things that happened.

I am enclosing some of my snaps and I should like to see yours.

Again, let me thank you both for giving me the time of my life.

Yours sincerely,
Peggy.

Letter Inviting a Friend to Stay in a Country House

Cranford,
Middle Haven,
Devonshire.
August 3rd, 19—.

My dear Beryl,

You have learned, I believe, from Mother that we are all down here, enjoying ourselves immensely.   The weather, so far, has been perfect and the sea air is doing us untold good. Everything seems to be combining to make our holiday a right royal success.

But my point in writing is this ı Will you come and join us ? Indeed, I will not ask the question, but express the command ı You must come and join us.

Come and stay a fortnight and come as soon as ever you can. I feel sure you will have an enjoyable time and will be all the better for the fresh air.

Don't trouble to bring a whole wardrobe full of dresses ı nobody dresses for dinner and life is absolutely free and easy. As you know, Father is keen on golf and we play a kind of mongrel game on the sands, so perhaps you would do well to bring your clubs.

Scribble me a note saying when you will come. I need hardly add that Jim will be extremely angry if you fail us.

Yours sincerely,
Ethel.

Letter Accepting an Invitation to Stay at a Country House

5, Trelawny Terrace,
S.W.20.

August 5th, 19—

Dear Ethel,

I cannot tell you of the delight your letter gave me. It is more than kind of you to think of me, at a time when you are all enjoying yourselves so much.

I just need a lazy holiday by the sea, and you have planned one for me that fits in exactly with my dreams.

It will be nice to spend the time with your people, Jim notwithstanding.

I can arrive on Thursday next, reaching Middle Haven at 5.15 p.m. Is this convenient to you ?

Yours sincerely,
Beryl.

Letter Inviting a Friend to Stay with the Writer at the Seaside

Burton House,
Chestnut Avenue,
Torquay.
July 28th, 19—.

My dear Beryl,

It seems ages since I saw anything of you, and I am sure a fortnight down here would be very good for you. I am still more sure that it would be very good for me, and for all of us. So I want to know if you can arrange to pay us a little visit next month. You know, without my telling you, how delighted we shall all be to have you among us again.

We were all so very sorry to hear of Jack's accident ; I do hope he has quite got over it, and has no evil result left behind. Please give him our sincere and warm remembrances.

I expect you will find Milly and John grown nearly out of recognition ; they wish me to send their love, and are looking forward to seeing you next month. With my own keen anticipation of your visit, and much love.

Yours sincerely,
Ethel.

Letter Inviting a Friend to Stay in the Country

Hollyholme,
West Wellsbourne,
Warwickshire.
June 1st, 19—.

My dear Mary,

John asked me the other day if you were ever coming to see us again—it seems such a long time since we saw you. Can you come before the end of the month and give us a few weeks ? We shall both be so very pleased if you can.

The country is looking lovely now ; the banks along the Framley Road are covered with foxgloves nearly to the top of the hedges—they are a sight for sore eyes indeed—the hay will soon be cut ; and I want you to see our roses before they begin to go off. Does all that not tempt you ?

John is frightfully pleased with a new car he has bought lately, and I know he wants to drive you from the station so that you can admire it properly. I had to give you that little hint beforehand. Well, dear, just write and say which day will suit you—how about the 15th ? But name any day that is not too far off.

With every good wish and warm regard from both of us.

Yours sincerely,
Nelly.

Letter of Invitation for a Christmas Visit

The Doves,
Eckford, Kent.
Dec. 10th, 19—.

My dearest Sallie,

We all want you to come and help us to enjoy Christmas this year. Will you come on the 23rd and give us a week ? The boys come home that day, and if you can conveniently join their train, or, say, arrive about the same time, James can meet you all and bring your luggage together. But, if that does not quite fit in with your plans, never mind. Something else can be arranged.

We are having a children's party, a dance for the grown-ups and several other events during the week : so please don't think of refusing.

With love from us all,
Yours sincerely,
Kitty Pershore.

Letter of Invitation to a Christening

                    38, Pope's Drive,
                         Bankford,
                              Durham.
                                   April 8th, 19—.

Dear Mary,

Sunday, April 17th, is a red-letter day for Roy John. He is to be christened at St. Paul's Church, Bankford, at 2.30.

The interest you have shown in our son and heir leads Will and me to ask you if you would honour us with your presence at the ceremony.

We should like you to arrive between 1.30 and 2, and stay the rest of the day.

Will sends his kind regards.

                         Yours sincerely,
                              Patricia.

Letter Refusing the Previous

                    40, Byron's Avenue,
                         Bankford,
                              Durham.
                                   April 9th, 19—.

Dear Patricia,

I am sure you will forgive me when I tell you that I am unable to come to Roy John's christening.

Mother is far from well and I do not think I ought to leave her. She has been ailing, now, for some days and misses me when I am not with her.

It was kind of you to ask me and I am sure you know that, in happier circumstances, I should have been delighted to come.

My love to the baby.

                         Yours sincerely,
                              Mary.

III

LOVE, COURTSHIP AND MARRIAGE

Love Letters in General

Love letters are the most highly personal of all forms of correspondence, and it would be misleading to try to lay down any rules for this sort of writing. There is only one worth-while rule, and that is simply: "Be yourself." Write naturally and without any affectation. Do not try for any highly literary style, or your letters will look artificial. The best thing is to write as you talk to your loved one.

The only reason for restraint is the necessity of guarding against making a definite promise that you may not want to keep. Love is a matter of emotions, but marriage concerns reason as well; do not allow yourself to be carried away by emotions at the temporary sacrifice of your reason.

The normal rules for beginning and ending letters do not apply to love letters. Every couple have their own pet ways, and in fact originality is half the charm of a love letter. "My dearest Joe", "My darling Betty", or simply "Darling" are all good openings, provided that a sufficient degree of intimacy has been established to justify these endearments. The word "love" cannot well be left out of the ending, although the exact wording of this is entirely a matter of taste.

Do not overdo the endearments, or they will begin to lose their value. Send kisses by all means, but do not decorate half a page with x's, as this looks rather cheap and silly. Above all, do not put x's or cryptic letters on the backs of envelopes. A person receiving letters in envelopes decorated in this way may be subjected to great derision from his or her family, and it may have the opposite effect from that intended.

Here is quite an ordinary letter from a man to his girl-friend. They have already declared their love for each other, and although they are not formally engaged they have a definite though private understanding between themselves. The letter is just an example of one style of writing a love letter.

Love Letter from a Man

> 3, Chiswick Terrace,
> Bristol.
> March 18th, 19—.

Darling,

Monday again—and another black Monday, because I've got to wait five long days before I see you again. I should be feeling utterly miserable if I hadn't got so many wonderful hopes and memories to keep me company. And after all, it was only yesterday that we were together, so I really ought not to grumble.

Joan dearest, I tried to tell you last night how much I love you, and I don't think I got out a fraction of what I really meant. I thought I might make up for that in this letter—and now I'm even more stuck for words. I'll have another go next week-end !

As you will guess, I'm writing this in my lunch-hour, and old Smithy is peering over his specs, in a frightfully curious way, but trying hard not to let me know it. I wonder if he wrote letters like this to Mrs. S. a couple of hundred years ago ? It's hard to believe !

It's just on two now, so I must pack up and get back to the grindstone.   Good-bye, sweetheart.   I'll write again before Saturday.   And I'll think of you all the time.

> Your own loving
> Danny.

Letter in Reply to the Previous Example

> 340, Longland Road,
> Cheltenham.
> March 19th, 19—.

My dearest Danny,

Mummy is giving me some real old-fashioned looks over the breakfast table these days, and the postman is getting downright cheeky.   Daddy goes on reading the paper and pretends not to notice,—he is a dear—but I'm expecting him to ask you any moment now if your intentions are honourable.   You have been warned !

I hate to think of you sticking at your desk with only old Smith to keep you company.   You poor dear—but you aren't the only one, you know.   My desk isn't any more delightful than yours, and my old Jones is just as much a stick-in-the-mud as your old Smithy.   But he did remark what a nice brooch I was wearing this morning.   " Is it a new one, Miss Taylor ? " he asked in that dry way of his— and he was dying to know who had given it to me.

Danny, dearest, I'm just as fed up waiting for week-ends as you are, but I feel a lot better when I get your letters.   I've got quite a bundle now, and they've all been read scores of times.

You know I'm not very good at expressing my feelings, expecially in letters—but you do know that I love you, don't you, Danny ?   Because I do—oh, terribly.

> Your own,
> Joan.

Proposals for Marriage in General

Proposals for marriage are almost invariably made verbally, and this method is always preferable to writing. The reasons are obvious. Shyness is a poor excuse, and even a stammered proposal is more likely to be favourably received than a beautifully written letter. The man who writes instead of speaks because he fears a rebuff is more likely to get a rebuff this way.

Therefore, a proposal should be made by letter only when there are special circumstances that make a verbal proposal impossible. The most usual circumstance is a long distance between the two parties. If it is impossible to overcome this—as it may be, for example, when the separation is due to military service or overseas employment —then a letter is justified.

Courtship by correspondence, like the more normal form of courtship, should be done gradually, and the man should have led up to the proposal in previous letters. The girl should try to give him an idea of her feelings in her replies, so that he will not make a definite proposal unless he has reason to believe that it will be favourably received.

The form of the letter containing the proposal will naturally depend to a great extent on the tenor of the previous correspondence. The important thing is that there should not be any noticeable change of style, and therefore the following example should be modified with this in view.

Letter Proposing Marriage

P.O. Box No. 525
Bombay,
India.
June 4th, 19—.

My dearest Eileen,
I don't know how many times I have complained in my

letters about our continued separation, and I think that
you have guessed by now that there is a pretty deep reason
behind this complaint.   This separation is more irksome
at the moment than it has ever been, because, dearest, I
do not feel able to put off any longer asking you a question
that I had been hoping to put in different circumstances.
I think you know what is coming, so here it is : darling,
will you marry me ?

You know that I love you, and that since we parted
six months ago my feelings have got even stronger.   I
couldn't ask you then, because we hadn't known each
other long, and in any case I expected to be home again
soon.   I meant to wait until I got back—but I just can't.

I know that I can't offer you much—not even myself
yet awhile—and goodness knows how much longer I shall
be stuck out here.   But there must be an end of it soon,
and the waiting will be less dreary if I can think that the
end will be the beginning of a new life with you as my wife.

I don't suppose I should have put it quite this way if
you had been with me, but it isn't easy to express feelings
of this sort in a letter.   I only hope you can read between
the lines and guess just how much I really love and want
you.

Yours, for ever if you want me, darling,
Dick.

Letter in Reply to the Previous Example

49, Oakfields Road,
Bath.
June 12th, 19—.

My dearest Dick,

Oh, yes, yes, YES !

But that is just to confirm my telegram with the same
words, which you should get to-day or to-morrow.   This
Air Mail is much too slow for me.

Was it unmaidenly of me to send a wire snapping up

your proposal like that, before you had a chance to change your mind ? Well, I took the risk. I suppose I ought to have said, " This is so sudden," or some such rot, but the fact is that it was nothing of the kind. You gave me a pretty broad hint in your previous letter—and when I replied I tried to give you the green light. Now I'll make you vain and tell you that I phoned through the telegram five minutes after I got your last letter.

Dick, I know you can't name the day, and I'm as fed up about this separation as you are. It's no good asking you to be patient, because I'm terribly impatient myself. We must just hope and dream.

Mummy and Daddy are writing to you separately— they need a little time for this sort of thing—but I can tell you now they are very pleased. I can't tell you how I feel —at the moment I'm just in a flap with excitement, and can't even eat. Darling Dick, I love you so much.

I'll write again when I've calmed down a bit. Until then, dearest,

Yours for ever,
Eileen.

Letter not Accepting a Proposal of Marriage

49, Oakfields Road,
Bath.
June 12th, 19—.

My Dear Dick,

You have paid me the greatest compliment any girl can receive, and the least I can do is to give you my answer promptly and frankly. I am writing by return; and, Dick, I am afraid the answer is no.

Reading your letter made me feel very guilty. It never occurred to me that you were leading up to this in your previous letters, and if I seemed to give you encouragement I assure you it was not intended. If we had been seeing each other instead of just writing I'm sure this would never have happened.

I owe you a reason at least for this refusal. It would be easy for me to say that we didn't know each other long enough, or that I'm not really sure about my feelings towards you. But that would be unfair. It might make you go on wasting your hopes on me ; and they would be wasted.

Dick, please don't take it too much to heart when I tell you bluntly that I shall never be your wife. I like you tremendously—more than any other man I know. But I'm not in love with you ; and—now don't be hurt—I never shall be.

Dick, I like and admire you, and I'm not worth your regrets. I've risked hurting your feelings because I don't want you to waste your time hoping that I'll change. I know I shan't. And I know you'll find someone much better fitted to be your wife than I am.

I hope you will always think of me as

Your very sincere friend,
Eileen.

Letter Postponing an Answer to a Proposal of Marriage

49, Oakfields Road,
Bath.

June 12th, 19—.

My Dear Dick.

I have just received your letter asking me to marry you, and now I'm expected to write back yes or no. Dick, I can't. I like you tremendously—you know that ; but I honestly don't know whether I love you. I didn't know you long enough while you were still in England, and I shan't really know how I feel until I see you again.

The other side of the picture is that you may find that I'm not quite all you imagine now that you can't see me, and I should hate you to come back and find that you didn't love your fiancée after all.

If I seemed to encourage you to make a proposal, I'm sorry. I didn't mean to.

I know that this " she didn't say yes, didn't say no " business is unsatisfactory, and I know that a time may come when I shall regret it. But I can't see any alternative.

May I make a suggestion ? Let's go on writing to each other as before, and see how it works out. But no ties yet. If either of us meets anyone else, the other has no claim.

A last word, Dick. I haven't met anyone else yet. If I do I'll tell you at once. I expect you to do the same— for this is my risk as well as yours.

Yours ever,
Eileen.

(*A letter such as the above should only be written if the writer sincerely means every word of it. In the interests of herself as well as of her lover a girl should never postpone a definite answer to a proposal if she can possibly help it.*)

Letter to a Girl-Friend Congratulating her on an Engagement

53, Locksley Mansions,
S.W.21.

March 31st, 19—.

Dear Betty,

I have heard whispers north, south, east and west, linking your name with a certain gentleman of military bearing. And, to-day, I have been told outright that you and he are engaged.

Let me be one of the first to offer you my congratulations. Needless to say, he is a very lucky man and he, too, is to be congratulated.

You will make a wonderful wife when the time comes,

and I can imagine you presiding over a delightful household to which, I trust, I may at times be invited.

I hope you will both be very happy.

Yours sincerely,
Brenda.

Letter of Congratulation to a Girl on her Engagement

Hannington House,
West Shelford.
July 8th, 19—.

My dear Jennie,

I must send you a line to tell you how glad I am to learn of your engagement to Willie Parminter. He is a great friend of my cousin Arthur, and we all like him so much. Arthur told my husband yesterday and I felt that I must write at once, because we are really so glad both for him and for you. Will you come and see me when you can and tell me all about it, and if any time is fixed yet ? Of course, I want to know everything at once. Give my love to your mother. God bless you, my dear, and with fondest love,

Yours ever,
Delia.

Letter to a Girl-Friend Congratulating her on an Engagement

The Six-Litre Motor Club,
Piccadilly, W.1.
April 3rd, 19—.

Dear Katherine,

When I turned over the pages of the " Daily Telegraph " at breakfast to-day I came to a notice about a certain Miss Katherine Birtwistle and some fellow who was evidently born under a lucky star. The notice told me that you have just become engaged.

Well, Katherine, my congratulations to you, and may this event open a new chapter of happiness in your life !

There is no doubt that your fiancé is fortunate indeed. I am sure he must be a good chap, for have I not told you a thousand times that your taste in all things is impeccable ?

I wish you every happiness.

Yours sincerely,
David.

Letter Congratulating a Mother on the Engagement of her Daughter

364, Sloan Drive,
S.W.1.
May 15th, 19—.

Dear Mrs. Durrant,

I was delighted to read in to-day's " Daily Telegraph " of the engagement of your daughter Joan to Mr. Egremont.

I am writing to congratulate both you and Joan and I trust she is and will be very happy. It is certainly something to make you feel proud.

My husband joins with me in sending our kind regards both to you and to Mr. Durrant.

Yours very sincerely,
Mary Florence Barker.

Letter of Congratulation to a Mother on the Engagement of her Daughter

3, Bilchester Terrace,
W.1.
July 3rd, 19—.

Dear Mrs. Drake,

May I, as an old friend, send you my congratulations,

on Cicely's engagement to Captain Blake, which I saw announced in " The Times " yesterday ? It is, I am sure, a source of pleasure to you all, and as Captain Blake has been known to you for so long, you must feel quite happy about the future of your daughter.

Do give my love and very kindest wishes to Cicely. I feel sure it is a real love match, and that it promises every happiness for both of them.

With very kindest regards from John and myself.

Yours sincerely,
Margaret Roberts.

Letter from a Man to his Fiancée who has been Angry with him

78, Marchmont Drive,
Gloucester Rd.,
S.W.3.
Sept. 8th, 19—.

My dearest Eva,

We've always agreed to be straight with each other, and I'm not going to pretend to be a penitent sinner now, because I don't feel one. You were cross with me, and as I told you, I thought you were unfair. I still think so— though I realize that I did not help matters by the way I took it.

I don't mind admitting that I've felt pretty fed up with life since our row. I want to make it up—but I know you wouldn't think much of me if I tried to win you back by pretending to take all the blame. I reckon it's about fifty-fifty, and I hope you'll agree to forget the whole thing existed.

Darling, I love you as much as I ever did. When can I come round and kiss and make up ?

Your loving
Bernard.

(The writer of this letter does not hide the fact that he thinks

his fiancée was unfair, but he is wise enough to realize that there is another side to it.   He is also wise in not begging to be taken back ; a happy marriage would not result from that sort of attitude.)

Letter in Reply to the Previous Example

49, Doncaster Street,
N. 20.
Sept. 9th, 19—.

My dearest Bernard,

You've made me feel an absolute pig.   I've been trying to write to you ever since Saturday, and it was only silly false pride that prevented me.   It would have served me right if I'd lost you.

I don't agree that the blame was fifty-fifty, or anything like that.   It was my fault—but if it's any consolation to you, I've felt utterly miserable ever since.

I think you're a darling, and I don't deserve you. Please come as fast as you can for the make-up kiss.

Your loving
Eva.

(The writer of this letter has the sense to appreciate the gesture made by her fiancé, and her letter is his reward for making the gesture.   By good sense on both sides the quarrel is ended.)

Letter from a Man after a Lovers' Quarrel

137, Meadfoot Road,
Bradley,
Devonshire.
July 9th, 19—.

Darling,

Will you forgive—and forget ?

I was a fool last night, and I know it.   I can't imagine why I said what I did, and I am kicking myself for being such an idiot.

This is the first time we have quarrelled. I am determined that it will be the last. I've never felt so miserable in my life.

When may I come and see you again ?

Your loving
Fred.

Letter in Reply to the Previous Example

68, Chesserton Road,
Bradley,
Devonshire.
July 10th, 19—.

My dearest Fred,

It is forgotten as far as I am concerned. I can't forgive you, because you were not the only one to blame. It takes two to make a quarrel, and I played my part too.

As you say, it was our first quarrel, and I'm with you in making it the last. I was feeling very miserable until your letter came.

Please come round as quickly as you can.

Your loving
Pam.

Letter from a Lady to her Son's Fiancée

Ballington Grange,
Denton.
Sep. 12th, 19—.

My dear Patricia,

Jack has written and told me of his great happiness in his engagement to you, but I feel that I cannot properly enter into his feelings until I have met you and welcomed you as my new daughter.

Jack tells me that he can get away from the office for a few days on the 18th, so I am writing to ask you whether you could come to stay with us on that day, so that we may all get to know you.

When next my husband is in town, he will make a point of calling upon your parents.

Jack will only be able to stay for a few days, but if you can arrange to make quite a long visit, we shall not grudge giving you up wholly to him while he is with us, as then we can have you to ourselves after his return to town.

Myra and Janet send their love and say they are most anxious to meet you, so do try to come.

Yours sincerely,
Mary Woodrow.

Letter Written by a Fiancée on being Invited to Visit the Man's House

14 Castle Street,
Hendon, N.W.
Sep. 14th, 19—.

My dear Mrs. Woodrow,

I think it is so very kind of you to write and ask me to visit you—I have asked my parents and they are quite willing to let me come on the 18th, and I need not tell you how delighted I shall be to meet you.

Mother says that the length of my visit must be left open, because if I don't behave myself, you will want to send me home. But I'm sure you're too kind-hearted to do that, however much I may deserve it.

I do hope you won't be disappointed when you see me, as I'm just an ordinary girl ; there's nothing special at all about me except that I really love Jack and pray I may be good enough to make him a good wife. So please don't expect too much from me or you will be dreadfully disappointed. May I send my love to Myra and Janet ?

Yours sincerely,
Patricia.

Letter from a Lady Breaking Off an Engagement

Burnside,
Haverfield,
Hunts.

July 8th, 19—.

Dear Jim,

I am writing to ask you to do a thing which I fear will give you pain, but which, after serious thought, I have decided will be best for us both. I wish you to free me from my engagement.

I will be perfectly frank with you. I now know that I never really loved you, and that it was the ardour of your love for me more than any true affection on my part which made me consent to marry you.

Here let me say that if ever a woman respected a man, I do you, for I know your qualities.

But respect is not love, and marriage without love would to me seem a mockery.

I think you understand me well enough to believe that I am not the kind of girl to make such a decision lightly, especially realising, as I do, how much it means to you.

So, forgive me if I have hurt you, and do allow me to consider myself always

Your sincere friend,
Mary.

Letter Breaking Off an Engagement

36, Ditton Hill Lane,
Charlton,
Stafford.

January 15th, 19—.

Dear Harry,

This is a very unfortunate letter to have to write and you may be sure that I have given it many bitter hours, if not days or weeks, of consideration.

The fact is I have come to the conclusion that we are not suited to each other, and to marry in these circumstances would be folly.

I think, then, that the only sensible plan is for us to part and, accordingly, I am asking you to release me from our engagement.

You have always been splendid to me and I admire you tremendously ; but, frankly, I have come to feel that it is not love that has brought us together.

I know this will hurt you and it is hurting me to write it ; but we must be sensible and face up to the facts as they are.

Yours sincerely,
Dora.

Letter Breaking Off an Engagement

36, Ditton Hill Lane,
Charlton,
Stafford.
January 15th, 19—.

Dear Harry,

The unfortunate incident of last Saturday evening is, I feel, the climax to a series of incidents which go to show that it would be folly for us to continue with our engagement.   On that account I am writing to ask you to release me.

It is now some months since I first began to feel we were drifting apart and that you no longer cared for me as you did formerly.

We have had many good times together and I shall always look back on them with pleasure ; but our future, I am sure, lies in different directions.

For these reasons, I am bound to say—good-bye and good luck.

Yours sincerely,
Dora.

Letter Breaking Off an Engagement

36, Ditton Hill Lane,
Charlton,
Stafford.

Dear Harry,   January 15th, 19—.

In all the circumstances I must definitely break off our engagement. It would be futile to go over all the points on which we have disagreed, and it would only serve to hurt us both. Please understand that this is final.

Yours sincerely,
Dora.

Letter Regarding a Broken Engagement

36, Ditton Hill Lane,
Charlton,
Stafford.

Dear Harry,   January 15th, 19—.

I must thank you for your letter. Unfortunately, I cannot reconsider my decision—it was final.

Yours sincerely,
Dora.

(In all cases of this nature, the dignified thing is to write nothing that will hurt more than necessary. It is very seldom advisable to argue about the facts or to set out the details at length. Though the writer may be burning with indignation, she merely states that she is withdrawing from the engagement, and leaves the case at that.)

Letter from a Man Breaking Off an Engagement

6, Woodside Park,
Woodside,
Essex.

Dear Phyllis,   July 8th, 19—.

It is with great reluctance that I am about to perform what I feel to be a duty to you and to myself.

I have to tell you that I realize that I no longer love you.   Indeed, I am not certain that I ever did—in the way you so well deserve to be loved.

What can I say in explanation ? Only this : you are such a charming person that, quite unconsciously, you draw others to yourself almost against their will. Any man thrown constantly in your society, as I have been, might, after a time, imagine that he loved you.

But circumstances have lately revealed to me the true feeling I have for you—and I am very sure it is not love.

I do not think I should have had the courage to tell you this, were it not that I have never been whole-heartedly certain of your affection for myself.

You see, it is second nature with you to be gracious and kind to all men, and this fact may have deceived me.

I pray it is so, and that in releasing me from the engagement there will be no lasting sorrow on your part ; only, as with myself, a passing regret.

While wishing you abundant happiness in the future, may I ask you always to think of me as

Your sincere friend,
Alfred.

Letter from a Man Offering his Fiancée her Freedom

The Boulders,
Cortland's Drive,
Hexavon.
June 8th, 19—.

My dearest Bertha,

This is a difficult letter to write.   The facts are that, of late, I have been wondering if you care for me as you used to do.   I may be entirely wrong, and I sincerely hope I am, but on a number of occasions I have noticed little incidents which seemed to show that my presence displeased you.

I can honestly say that my affection has not changed

or grown less in any way and that I want you as much as I ever did. But this is the point ! It is folly to go on if you are growing cold. I want you to be happy and I want you to be happy with me, but unless you can assure me that you are not changing, it would be better to call our engagement off.

So, please Bertha, do be perfectly honest and tell me if I am right or wrong.

Yours ever,
Ken.

Letter from a Lady to a Gentleman asking him to Refrain from Pursuing his Unwanted Attentions

38, Cambridge Gardens,
S.E.32.
July 18th, 19—.

S. Reynold Esq.

Dear Sir,

I find it necessary to write to you on a matter which has caused me some concern lately. I refer to your persistent and, to me, distasteful attentions.

I do not think I have ever given you any encouragement, and I am hoping that, on reading this expression of my feelings, your good taste will prompt you to desist from what I cannot but consider an embarrassing annoyance.

Yours truly,
Beryl Ross.

Letter Requesting a Man to Cease his Attentions, from the Girl's Father (Friendly Attitude)

38, Cleveland Rd.,
N.24.
July 8th, 19—.

Dear Mr. Boyd,

I am sorry that things have happened as they have.

In all the circumstances it will be best if you do not see Marie again.

It is unfortunate and I know this will cause you pain, but having discussed the position thoroughly with her, it is clear to me that her mind is made up. Therefore, please make things as easy as you can.

My wife and I hope you will forget Marie as soon as possible.

Yours sincerely,
Arthur M. Brown.

Letter Requesting a Man to Cease his Attentions, from the Girl's Father (Annoyed)

38, Cleveland Rd.,
N.24.
July 8th, 19—.

S. Boyd Esq.,
Sir,

I am astonished to learn that you have not yet understood that my daughter has no desire to be subjected to your attentions, and I am writing to point out again that she does not wish to see or speak to you. Accordingly, I must ask you to desist from annoying her. There are ways of forcing you to cease, and I shall not hesitate to use them if you make it necessary.

Yours faithfully,
A. M. Brown.

Letter from a Man Announcing his Marriage

Knebworth,
Clayton Hill,
Hoddesdon.
July 25th, 19—

Dear Wilfred,

At last the happiest man in the world is writing to

tell you that he has married the sweetest girl on earth.

I can see your knowing smile at this—but you do not yet know by personal experience what is meant by " the joys of matrimony."

Think of it, old boy ! After a hard day's work, to return to my own home, neat, bright, and comfortable— and, above all, presided over by a cheerful ministering angel.

If you are in any way sceptical, come and see us at the very earliest opportunity. Be prepared to stay a day or so ; and I am convinced you will leave a convert, and with a firm resolve to do likewise.

With very pleasant recollections of the many " good times " we have had together in my bachelor days, and kindest regards from Isabel,

Yours ever,
Will.

Letter of Congratulation to a Man on his Marriage (Written by a Man)

Savoy Court,
W.C.2.
July 27th, 19—

Dear Will,

Your very welcome note, announcing your marriage, reached me this morning. Hearty congratulations, old chap !

Not yet having a very intimate acquaintance with the lady, I will take all you have said of her for granted.

Your kind invitation I will gladly accept, and you may expect me over next Saturday.

My kindest regards to Cicely.

Yours ever,
Wilfred.

Letter of Congratulation to a Man on his Marriage
(Written by a Man)

53, Clark's Hill,
Horbury,
N.17.

April 18th, 19—.

Dear David,

You are to be congratulated. Fancy you being married! I can't realise it.

I have only just heard the news and, as you see, I am not wasting a moment in rushing in with my best wishes for a really happy married life.

You always were a lucky chap and now I suppose you have found the sweetest girl under the sun. I cannot imagine your doing anything else, for you always have known what is good.

And, let me say, I think there is not one but two people who must be congratulated.

May I offer Mrs. David Jones my kind regards?

Yours sincerely,
Arthur.

Letter of Congratulation to a Man on his Marriage
(Written by a Lady)

31, Selwyn Gardens,
Blandford.

April 16th, 19—.

Dear Rupert,

All the nice men are getting married, and now I hear that you have joined the noble army. My mother and I wish you both a great deal of happiness and we send our congratulations.

We should love to meet Audrey, and so we hope you will bring her to see us one day very soon.

There is a small gift enclosed from Mother and me which we are sending with our best wishes to you both.

Yours sincerely,
Doreen.

Letter of Thanks for a Wedding Present

38, Victoria Mansions,
W.21.
June 18th, 19—.

Dear Violet,

It was sweet of you to send us such a lovely wedding present. I really don't know how I can thank you. Derek was here last night and he is as pleased with it as I am.

We are looking forward to having you with us on the great day and, if you take my advice, you will follow our example at no distant date.   I am terribly busy, but wonderfully happy.

Thank you so very much.

Yours sincerely,
Sally.

Letter of Congratulation on a Silver Wedding

14, Grant Street,
Angmering,
Sussex.
June, 10th, 19—

My Dear Joe,

It is just twenty-five years to-morrow since that memorable day when I played the Best Man at your wedding. Afterwards I proposed the health of Mary and yourself, and expressed the hope that you would have many happy years together.

Now you and Mary will be celebrating the occasion together, and you have every reason to feel pleased with yourselves.   I know of only one other couple who have been as happy together as you—and you can guess whom I mean.

Joan joins me in wishing you many more years of happiness together. We enclose a little souvenir of the occasion —and I hope that we shall be able to send you another one in gold in twenty-five years' time.

Yours ever,
Tom.

Letter in Reply to the Previous Example

29, Neil Street,
W.4.
June 12, 19—

My dear Tom,

How very kind of you to think of us on our Silver Wedding day. Your charming gift is in a place of honour on our sideboard—only a foot or so away from the present you gave us twenty-five years ago, which has lasted as well as we have.

It was almost exactly three years after that day that I had the pleasure of being your Best Man, and I look forward to returning your congratulations when you join us in this silvered respectability. I know that you and Joan are our nearest rivals for the Dunmow Flitch.

Mary joins me in thanking you both and wishing you every happiness in the future.

Yours ever,
Joe.

Letter of Congratulation on a Golden Wedding

The Haven,
Seaburn,
Dorset.
3rd Nov., 19—.

Dear Mr. and Mrs. Fox,

To-morrow is the fiftieth anniversary of your wedding

day, and my wife and I wish to offer you our sincere congratulations.

No doubt you will be casting your minds back to various incidents in your married life and we are sure the thoughts will afford you a great deal of pleasure.   You have indeed had a fortunate time together, but that is merely what you both deserve.

May life continue to be happy for you, and may you both enjoy each other's company for many, many years to come.

Yours sincerely,
B. H. Thomas.

IV

SITUATIONS, APPOINTMENTS, ETC.

Letter Applying for a Post as Typist

38, West Park Terrace,
Hamford.

Sep. 3rd, 19—.

The Secretary,
The Atlas Glassworks, Ltd.

Dear Sir,

In answer to your advertisement in this morning's " News Chronicle," may I submit this application for the post of typist which is vacant ?

I am 18 years of age, have just left the —— School, and have passed the G.C.E. (or C.S.E.) Examination. I can write shorthand at a speed of one hundred words a minute, and have a fairly good grasp of French. I am enclosing copies of three testimonials.

This letter is a specimen of my typing.

Yours faithfully,

Susan Hellier.

(Naturally, as the post is for a typist, the letter submitted must be a perfect example of typing.)

Letter Applying for a Business Post

77, Gerald Crescent,
Somerleigh,
Maidstone.

July 18th, 19—.

The Secretary,
The Empire Trading Concern.

Dear Sir,

I beg to offer my services for the post which you have advertised as vacant in to-day's " Daily Telegraph."

Enclosed I am submitting a summary of my qualifications and experience, together with copies of three recent testimonials.

In particular, I should like to draw your attention to
.. ..
(place here any special qualifications.)

I should be pleased to call upon you at almost any time by appointment.

Yours faithfully,
G. Williams.

Letter Applying for a Junior Post in an Office

13, Valley Road,
Beechcroft,
Surrey.

Oct. 3rd, 19—.

The Secretary,
Messrs. Axford & Co., Ltd.

Dear Sir,

I am told that you have a vacancy in your office for a junior clerk. May I offer myself for the post?

At present I am a pupil in the sixth form of the County School, Beechcroft, and I want to enter upon a business career.

Last summer, I passed the G.C.E. (or C.S.E.) Examination and my Headmaster tells me that he will be able to answer favourably any questions regarding my character.

I am $17\frac{1}{2}$ years of age.

If you could grant me an interview, I should be pleased to call whenever convenient to you.

> Yours faithfully,
> R. G. Norman.

Letter in Reply to an Advertisement Respecting a Vacant Post

> 33, Ferndale Mansions,
> Ealing, W.5.
> July 8th, 19—.

Box 354,
c/o " The Daily Journal."

Dear Sir,

In answer to your advertisement in " The Daily Journal " of to-day's date, I wish to offer myself for the vacant post.

On an accompanying sheet I have set out those of my qualifications which, I think, will help you most in considering my application.   But I should like to mention specially that I ....
....

If you will allow me, I should be glad to call upon you at any time which is convenient to you.

> Yours faithfully,
> G. Gregory.

(Fill in the blank space with particulars of some special qualifications and do not forget to enclose the additional sheet with full particulars in column form.)

Letter Applying for a Post

68, Middleford Rd.,
Templeton.
March 16th, 19—.

G. A. Barrow, Esq.,
The Tile and Timber Works,
Templeton.

Dear Sir,

Mr. Arthur Burton, with whom I believe you are well acquainted, has suggested that I should write to you as, he says, you often have vacancies in your works.

Until two months ago, I was a —— at the Crown Works, and since that factory closed down I have been unemployed.

If you could give me work of any kind, it would be a great help to me.

Mr. Burton knows me well and would answer for my character.

Yours faithfully,
A. Page.

Letter In Answer to a Request for an Interview

68, Middleford Rd.,
Templeton.
March 20th, 19—

G. A. Barrow Esq.,
The Tile and Timber Works.

Dear Sir,

I wish to thank you for your letter of March 19th, in which you request me to call for an interview.

I shall be pleased to wait on you, as directed, on Thursday next at 3.15 p.m.

Yours faithfully,
A. Page.

(It is very important that such a letter should be sent. First, it shows that the one seeking the post pays attention

to details ; it reminds the receiver of the engagement, and it effectively checks any mistake that could be made about the time and the date.)

Letter Applying for a Post of Typist

68, Courtwood Road,
Hornsey, N.8.
February 6th, 19—

Box No. 541,
c/o " The Daily Argus."

Dear Sir,

In reply to your advertisement in this morning's " Daily Argus," I wish to submit this application for the post you mention as being vacant.

I am now working in the office of a Building Firm in Chelsea.

My age is 24½.

I am able to type quickly and accurately.

I can write shorthand (105 words a minute).

I do much of the work of book-keeper.

I have excellent references.

Yours faithfully,
Eileen Meyrick.

Letter Seeking an Office Appointment

66, Windsor Avenue,
Leeds.
Sep. 3rd, 19—

James Braid, Esq.,
Sales Dept.,
Messrs. F. R. Sims & Son, Ltd.,
Leeds.

Dear Sir,

I understand that the post of Secretary-Typist will shortly fall vacant in your department, and I wish to offer myself for the position.

I am 23 years of age, and my qualifications are as under :

Speed, Shorthand : 120 words per minute.

Speed, Typing : 40 words per minute.

Familiar with most standard machines, and the use of the Dictaphone.

Have had 5 years' experience in general correspondence work, including drafting from rough notes, keeping registers and card index ; and have gained a thorough knowledge of office routine.

My present employer sympathises with my desire to improve my position, and is willing that you should refer to him as to my abilities.

Trusting that you will grant me an interview,

I am, Sir,

Yours faithfully,

Edith Fildes.

Letter Applying for the Post of Traveller

Hollydene,

Collingwood Rd.,

Norton.

August 27th, 19--

Box 3998,

" The Daily Mercury."

Dear Sirs,

Will you consider my application for the post advertised in this morning's " Daily Mercury " ?

I am 26 years of age and in good health.

I have travelled Sussex for three years.

I am an ex-public schoolboy.

My present line is ——.

I enclose copies of three recent testimonials.

My weekly turnover, at present, averages ——.

Yours faithfully,

B. Gray.

(*Applications, such as this, which are crisp and to the*

point often draw attention when longer and more involved ones are passed over.)

Letter from a Traveller, Offering to Act as Agent for a Firm

167, Grove Avenue,
Broomfields,
York.
November 19th, 19—

Messrs. R. Perry, Ltd.

Dear Sirs,

Every week I have to call on fifty confectioners in the Northern Counties. I am told that you have no travellers in this area. As your lines do not in any way compete with those in which I am interested, I could represent your goods to our mutual advantage.

Would it be possible for you to appoint me as your representative for this territory ?

Yours faithfully,
S. Cathcart.

Letter Applying for the Post of Store-Cashier

38, Fallowfield Rd.,
Litchfield,
N.W.30.

3—8—. .

The Manager,
Messrs. Stoker & Co., Ltd.

Dear Sir,

I am submitting this application for the post of store-cashier, which your advertisement in " The Daily Post " says is vacant.

At present, I am cashier in the hardware department of Messrs. Timson's Store. I am 21 years of age and am earning £66 per week. My reason for applying to you is that you are offering a higher wage and better prospects.

My manager says that I may truthfully claim to be quick and accurate.   Enclosed is a testimonial which he has written for me.

I have only had three days' absence in the last three and a half years.

Yours faithfully,
Jean Jeavons.

Letter Applying for a Post in a Chain-Store

538, Pemberton Road,
New Southgate,
N.11.
Oct. 30th, 19—.

Box 398,
" The Morning Argus."

Dear Sir,

I have read your advertisement in to-day's " Morning Argus " and wish to apply for one of the vacant posts which you mention.

I have had five years' sales experience in two different firms.   Though the class of trade with which I dealt was slightly different from yours, I think my experience would be valuable to me in the new work you describe.

My ambition is not so much to obtain a good salary now as to secure a post which would give scope for my energies, and enable me to gain advancement later on.

Yours faithfully,
S. Beechcroft.

Letter Applying for a Post of Saleswoman

59, Grosvenor Rd.,
N.23.
Sep. 14th, 19—.

The Staff Superintendent.

Dear Madam,

In answer to your advertisement in this morning's

" Daily Leader," I wish to offer you my application for the vacant post of shoe saleswoman.

I am at present employed in a high-class shoe dealer's establishment as a junior.   There are no prospects for me, since the firm has but one shop and there are three assistants senior to me.   That is my only reason for seeking a change.

My age is 24, I am 5 ft. 6½ ins. and have good health. I am anxious to get on and believe I should prove thoroughly satisfactory.   I enclose two testimonials and my present employer will give me a good reference. (Insert his name, address and telephone number.)

I should be pleased to call on you, if desired.

Yours faithfully,
Winifred Hobson.

Letter Applying for a Post (American Style)

64, Palmers Road,
Totterton,
Church End,
N.3.
Oct. 28th, 19—

The Staff Manager,
  King St., W.18.
    Dear Sir,
      Re—Your advertisement in " The Newsbox."

I believe I am the man you are looking for.   I know a good deal about furniture, have been selling it for five years and can sell yours.   If you will try me on a commission-basis, without salary, for a month, I am certain you will be ready to put me on the permanent staff at the end of the time.

I am a hard worker and don't watch the clock.   Some people call me a live wire.

May I come and help to increase your sales ?

Yours faithfully,

G. Gardner.

(Many people would drop this letter in the waste-paper basket ; but, on the other hand, many would read it twice. They would argue that the writer had " cheek " of the kind that would help in selling and they might seriously consider the application.)

Letter Seeking a Post in a Factory

55, Davidson Avenue,
Manchester.

Sep. 18th, 19—.

The Concrete Construction Co.
King's Rd.,
Manchester.

Dear Sirs,

I have seen in to-day's " Manchester Guardian " your advertisement for a ——, and I wish to offer you my services in that capacity.

I enclose a summary of my qualifications and experience, together with copies of three recent testimonials.   The originals of these, I shall be pleased to send or bring personally for your inspection, should you be disposed to consider my application.

The persons mentioned as references have assured me of their willingness to speak for me as regards character. They have both known me for several years.

Yours faithfully,

James Smith.

(This will serve as an application for almost any kind of post.   Be careful to enclose the testimonial copies.)

Letter from a Chauffeur Seeking a Post

3, Streatley Rd.,
Sydenham Rise,
S.E.23.
January 3rd, 19—.

George Barker Esq.

Dear Sir,

I wish to apply for the post of chauffeur as advertised in the " Telegraph " this morning. I spent two years in the S—— Motor Company's works and have a thorough knowledge of all modern makes of cars, and can do all running and ordinary repairs.

For the last eighteen months I have been in the service of Mr. James Smith, of Bowden Manor, Croydon, but he is now going abroad. He has given me a good testimonial, a copy of which I enclose.

I shall be pleased to call upon you at any time you may find convenient.

Yours faithfully,
James Hogg

Letter Thanking an Employer for a Post that is not being Accepted

3, Streatley Rd.,
Sydenham Rise,
S.E.13.
January 18th, 19—.

George Barker Esq.

Dear Sir,

I greatly appreciated the trust you placed in me by offering me the vacant post of chauffeur.

By a curious coincidence, I was offered to-day a similar position at a higher wage. I feel it a duty to my family that I should accept the better wage, and I have done so.

Therefore, it is with regret that I must withdraw my application to you, but I should like to thank you, none the less.

Yours faithfully,
James Hogg.

Letter Enquiring for a Business Character

THE LOUGHTON WORKS
Muchford,
Hants.

July 18th, 19—.

Messrs. Mayford & Co., Ltd.

Dear Sirs,

We have just had an interview with Mr. Arthur Meyrick, who has applied for the post of cashier with us.

He has given your name as a reference, stating that he has served you for three years in a similar capacity.

Would you favour us with a note stating whether you consider him a suitable man to appoint ?   Any information you may be able to give us will be valued and treated in confidence.

Yours faithfully,
G. R. Rhead
(Secretary).

Letter in Reply to the Previous Example

MAYFORD & CO., LTD.,
Southampton.

July 19th, 19—.

G. R. Rhead Esq.,
The Loughton Works,
Muchford, Hants.

Dear Sir,

In reply to your letter of July 18th, I am instructed

by our Managing Director to inform you that Mr. Arthur Meyrick has filled the post here as Cashier for a period of three years.

During this time he has proved eminently successful and capable, and his only reason for wishing to leave us is to seek a more remunerative post.

Should he be favoured with your appointment, our Company will be sorry to lose his services ; but, at the same time, it has no wish to stand in the way of his advancement.

Yours faithfully,
S. G. Smith
(Secretary).

Alternative Letter to the Former

MAYFORD & CO., LTD.,
Southampton.

July 19th, 19—.

G. H. Rhead Esq.,
The Loughton Works,
Muchford, Hants.

Dear Sir,

Our Managing Director, Mr. K. Staines, wishes me to thank you for your letter of July 18th, enquiring about an applicant's character.   He wonders if it would be possible for you to call here, as he would like to have a chat with you on the subject.   If this is impossible, perhaps you could 'phone him ?

Yours faithfully,
S. G. Smith
(Secretary).

(*This form of reply is useful when it is felt that it would be unwise to set down on paper all that one wishes to say.*)

Letter Asking for a Testimonial

3, Burton Villas,
Pemberton,
Leeds.

Nov. 8th, 19—.

S. Fentiman Esq.

Dear Sir,

I recently applied for the post of Garage Manager at the Ace of Hearts Garage, Pemberton. Yesterday the owners wrote and said that my application was being considered, but that they wished me to supply two recent testimonials.

As I believe you looked favourably on the standard of my work when I served under you, I am wondering whether you could help me by writing me a testimonial.

If you could do this I am sure it would advance my chances of securing the post, and I should be most grateful.

Yours faithfully,
Thomas Flaxman.

Letter Asking for a Reference

48, Cambridge Rd.,
High End,
Lexford.

Sep. 4th, 19—.

G. Browning Esq.

Dear Mr. Browning,

When I left school at the end of last term, you very kindly suggested that I might use your name when seeking a post. I am applying for the position of junior——in the Anglo-French Oil Company and have given your name as one of three references.

I understand that the Company may write to you and, in that event, I hope you will be able to speak well of me. The post is not a highly paid one, but it offers excellent prospects.

I should like to take this opportunity of thanking you for all you did for me while I was at school.

Yours sincerely,

N. Scott.

(It is only a matter of courtesy to tell the recipient that his or her name has been used as a reference.)

Letter Giving a Reference for a Maid

3, Bishop's Walk,
Hampton.

Jan. 3rd, 19—.

Dear Mrs. Larcombe,

In reply to your letter, dated Jan. 1st, I have much pleasure in recommending Joan Brassett. She was with me for three years and left last June to nurse her mother. I may say that I have a high opinion of her character and capabilities. She has a pleasant manner, is perfectly trustworthy, and extremely thoughtful.

Were I coming back to London, I should be quite prepared to re-engage her.

Yours faithfully,

Nancy French.

(The chief thing to avoid, when writing a testimonial for a person one can recommend, is excessive praise. When overdone, it is liable to have a repelling effect.)

Letter Recommending a Housekeeper

Wilkington Rectory,
Crowbury,
Sussex.

Jan. 14th, 19—.

Dear Mrs. Ullington,

I have pleasure in stating that, having known Mrs. Wilson and her varied circumstances intimately for the last thirty years, I have a very high opinion of her general

character and capabilities.   I believe her to be thoroughly
high-principled and trustworthy.

She brought up a family of four children, who are all a
credit to their home, and she was a devoted and faithful
wife.   After losing her husband, her children being then
all grown up, she took special lessons in cookery and
attended some domestic science lectures, and for the last
five years has acted as housekeeper for Lady Brown-
Sengsford, who, I believe, found her entirely satisfactory.
I knew her husband well, and her family ; they were
parishioners of mine for twenty years before her husband
died, and I had the opportunity of seeing a great deal of
Mrs. Wilson and of her husband and family, and I know
that I am not alone in the parish in my very high opinion
of her.

Yours faithfully,

A. B. Hemmings,

Rector of Wilkington.

Reply to an Answer to an Advertisement Regarding the Post of Nurse (Governess)

Norfolk Lodge,

Billington,

Lincolnshire.

May 6th, 19—.

Lady Foskett.

Madam,

I thank you for your reply to my advertisement
for post as head-nurse.   In my present engagement, which
I am leaving on the 15th of next month, I have had
entire charge of the nursery since the birth of the youngest
little girl, who is now five years old, and for whom Lady
Charles is engaging a French nursery governess.   There
are besides three older children—a boy who is now six

and a half years, and twins, a boy and girl eight years old. I have had one under-nurse, and an under-house-maid has had the care, under my direction, of the nurseries. I am glad to be able to say that the children are all thoroughly healthy, and have ailed but very little since I took charge of them.

Lady Charles is kind enough to say that she will be glad to recommend me ; I can also give other satisfactory references. I am naturally very fond of children, and have had to do with them all my life.

Before coming here I was second-nurse with the Honble. Mrs. Rhys, where there were four children in the nursery. I remained there for three years. I am thirty-two years of age, and have very good health. I shall be able to enter upon another engagement by the 31st of next month.

May I ask you to be so kind as to let me know as soon as possible if you would like to see me, as I have other answers to my advertisement ? Salary required, £— a year ; and if any special uniform is to be worn, £— a year for uniform.

Yours faithfully,
Marian Russell.

Letter Enquiring about the Character of a Nurse

Brussington Hall,
Northborough.

May 8th, 19—.

Dear Lady Charles,

I should be exceedingly obliged if you would kindly tell me what you think of Miss Marian Russell as a head-nurse. Is she thoroughly healthy, truthful, and trust-worthy ? Has her care of the nursery been satisfactory, and are the children happy in her care ? Miss Russell states that she has had charge of your nursery for five years, and that the children's health has been good during that time.   May I rely upon that statement, and can you thoroughly recommend Miss Russell as head-nurse ?

Yours sincerely,

Joan Foskett.

Letter Recommending a Private Governess

Haverstock Hall,
Rutlandshire.

July 8th, 19—.

Dear Mrs. Green,

I have much pleasure in recommending Miss Mary Jevons as private governess.   Miss Jevons lived with me for three years as governess to my two daughters, who are now twelve and thirteen years old, and my little boy, aged eight ; she gained the affection, respect and entire confidence of the children, and proved herself an excellent teacher, as is shown by all three children taking very good places in their schools—indeed, their French and English have been specially remarked upon by their present teachers.   It was with very great regret that I parted from Miss Jevons when other arrangements had to be made for the children.

Yours sincerely,

Alice Rainsforth.

Letter Requesting a Reference for a Governess

Four Ways,
Purley Way,
Surrey.

Sep. 10th, 19—.

Dear Mrs. Bennett,

I have been referred to you by Miss Elizabeth Gray,

who tells me that she was recently employed by you as governess to your girls.

I understand that she enjoyed your confidence for several years, and that you approved of her methods of training your daughters. I shall be greatly obliged if you would give me your opinion of her qualifications for a similar post in my home—especially as regards her moral influence over young children, and her powers as a musician.

I am sorry to trouble you, but should be glad to have a reply as early as possible.

Yours sincerely,

Sarah Ling.

Letter of Resignation from an Appointment

3, Ham Terrace,
Hamborough,
Lincolnshire.

August 15th, 19—.

G. A. Lindsey Esq.,
Messrs. Lindsey & Co., Ltd.

Dear Sir,

Will you kindly accept my resignation, to take effect on September 16th next ?

I have accepted a post with Messrs. Smith and Taylor, Ltd., of Merrowbridge and commence my duties there early in October.

I should like to take this opportunity of thanking you for all your favours in the past five years.

I regret leaving ; but the new post carries with it greater responsibilities, and I feel that they will help to advance me in my work.

Yours faithfully,

B. Mansbridge.

(*A suitable letter when the writer is leaving in an amicable manner.*)

Letter of Resignation from an Appointment

3, Ham Terrace,
Hamborough,
Lincolnshire.
August 15th, 19—.

Messrs. Lindsey & Co., Ltd.

Dear Sirs,

I beg to hand you my resignation, to take effect on September 16th next.

Yours faithfully,
B. Mansbridge.

(It is evident that such a letter is only suitable when the writer wishes to resign in a dignified manner, but is labouring under a grievance. Many would be tempted to add a few lines of abuse, but in the long run, the above is much better.)

V

HOME MATTERS

Letters dealing with what are essentially home matters come within this section.   But the sections on " Landlord and Tenant," " Invitations," etc. contain many letters that also apply to home matters.

Letter regarding the Absence of a Child from School

> 80, Fulwell Road,
> Fulham, S.W.6.
> March 3rd, 19—

The Headmistress.

Dear Madam,

My daughter Susan is returning to school to-day, after nearly a week's absence.   A few days ago she was vaccinated and soon developed a very painful arm. In the circumstances it seemed advisable to keep her at home.

She is much better now and I believe she will do what she can to make up for lost time.

> Yours faithfully,
>
> Jean Wormald.

Letter Asking for a Child's Homework to be Excused

66, Goldsmith Road,
Highfields,
Westerham,
Kent.

Feb. 19th, 19—.

The Headmistress.*

Dear Madam,

Would you kindly excuse the homework that Barbara should have done last night ?

Unfortunately, my daughter came home at tea-time with a bad headache and I thought it necessary for her to go to bed.   Thus, she was unable to do the work set.

Yours faithfully,*

Mary Simmonds.

(*If preferred, substitute the name of the Headmistress, and write " Yours sincerely," when the headmistress has been met or is known.)

Letter Explaining Absence from the Office

37, Brierfield Road,
Mitcham.

June 5th, 19—.

W. Griffiths Esq.,
Messrs. Pears, Wayward & Hope.

Dear Sir,

I am sorry to report that my daughter Gladys will be unable to come to the office on Monday, as she has sprained her ankle.

The doctor does not consider it serious, but thinks that forty-eight hours' rest will put it right.

She very much regrets the inconvenience she is causing you and trusts you will excuse her.

Yours faithfully,

Henry Jones.

Letter Explaining Absence

754, Grovers Lane,
Beckenham,
Kent.

Feb. 3rd, 19—

F. Grainger Esq.,
The London Sheet Metal Co., Ltd.
Dear Sir,

I trust you will excuse my non-attendance at work to-day; my wife's illness has taken a more serious turn, and I am compelled to remain at home for the present.

I hope to arrange matters so that I shall be able to appear as usual to-morrow, or the next day at the latest. Should anything unforeseen prevent my doing so, I will inform you.

Yours faithfully,
Edwin Mander.

Letter Regretting Absence from Work

Hill Top,
Burwash, Hythe.
February 3rd, 19—.

E. Angus Esq.
Dear Sir,

I much regret that I have not been able to reach the office this week. As my wife mentioned over the 'phone, I am suffering from an attack of lumbago and find it almost impossible to move. The doctor has come on alternate days and, in his opinion, I shall not be fit to return until next Monday.

I am exceedingly sorry to have caused you inconvenience, but it has been absolutely unavoidable.

Yours faithfully,
J. Faithful.

(*In letters of this kind, give some idea of the nature of the illness, but do not go into minute detail.*)

Letter Apologising for a Late Reply

> Mayfields,
> River Lane,
> Salisbury.
>
> Feb. 6th, 19—.

Dear Diana,

I owe you a very sincere apology. You wrote to me —weeks ago, and up till now your letter has remained unanswered. I don't care for excuses, but on this occasion, I trust you will listen to the one I am offering.

When your letter arrived.............................
....
....
....

In your letter, you asked...............................
....
....
....

In the circumstances, I do hope you will accept my apology and not think too badly of me.

> Yours sincerely,
> Cicely Appleton.

(*In the first space, give some reason for the delay in answering, such as absence from home, illness, loss of the address, etc.*)

Letter Congratulating a Friend on Passing an Examination

> 71, Hills Crescent,
> Cambridge.
>
> July 1st, 19—.

Dear Betty,

I have just heard that you have passed your examination with flying colours. May I offer you my heartiest congratulations ? It is an achievement of which you ought to be proud. Undoubtedly, you deserved to get through, for if anyone ever worked hard and denied herself pleasures, it was you.

Mother joins with me in singing your praises ! she says your parents ought to be proud of you ! moreover, she says she wishes she had a daughter who could gain such distinction and so bring honour to the family. I am afraid, however, that I was not built that way and, being deficient in scholarly qualities, must be content to envy the achievements of others.

You now deserve a good rest which I trust you will certainly have.

Yours ever,
Pamela.

Letter of Complaint to a Neighbour about the Damage Caused by a Dog, Cat, etc.

36, Seaview Lane,
Ferryford,
Sussex.
July 8th, 19—.

Dear Mr. Henslowe,

I am sorry to have to appear unneighbourly, but I must really ask you to do something about your dog. Recently it has made a practice of coming into my garden and doing a great deal of damage. It has ruined quite a number of plants and has done much to spoil the appearance of the flower beds.

I am afraid that none of this would have happened had your fences been in order.

Trusting that you will see to it that I am put to no further trouble,

Yours sincerely,
G. Ripon.

(With slight alteration, the same letter will serve for many other kinds of nuisances.)

Letter Questioning a Household Account

84, Brownlows Gardens,
Easterly.
Jan. 4th, 19—.

The General & District Gas Co.
Dear Sirs,

On receiving your account for the quarter's supply of gas, I was astonished to find that the bill was for so large an amount.

As the consumption indicated is far in advance of any previous quarter and as there is no reason for supposing that we have used more gas, I can only conclude that the meter is out of order.   Will you please be good enough to give the matter your earliest attention ?

Yours faithfully,
S. McDonald.

Letter to a Newsagent or any Daily Supplier

54, The Chase,
Kingsford,
Essex.
August 2nd, 19—

S. Boydell Esq.
Dear Sir,

As we shall be away on holiday for a short time, will you please stop the delivery of all morning papers after August 4th ?

We shall require the papers on August 4th.

Yours faithfully,
Arthur Reed.

(*Note that the date must be made quite clear.*)

Letter to the Local Builder-Repairer

48, Hunter's Lane,
Harringay,
N.22.

A. Burroughs Esq.   April 5th, 19—.
Dear Sir,

We have four or five sash lines that are broken and a door that needs repairing.

Could you send a man to attend to these things ? Please do not arrange for him to come on Monday before 12 noon, or on Tuesday after 3 p.m.

Yours faithfully,
Ada Champion.

A Letter of Rebuff

38, Longbridge Drive,
Westbrook.

L. Burns Esq.   August 3rd, 19—.
Sir,

In answer to your letter of August 2nd, I wish to state that I have nothing to add to my last communication.

I do not wish to appear discourteous, but I must decline to enter into further correspondence in the matter.

Yours faithfully,
A. K. Long.

Letter to a House Agent at the Seaside seeking Accommodation

68, Round Lane,
Boundary Rd.,
Heathfield.

June 30th, 19—.

Messrs. Beadmore & Long.
Dear Sirs,

Having seen your advertisement in " Dalton's

Weekly," I am writing to ask if you have, on your books, a furnished house which is available for the months of August and September ?

My requirements are :

— Bedrooms.
— Sitting-rooms.
— Attendance.
— Distance from sea, at most.
— Rent (inclusive).

Should you be able to send me a favourable reply, it shall have my immediate consideration.

Yours faithfully,
(Mrs.) A. B. Mitchell.

Letter Accepting Holiday Apartments

62, Bassett Rd.,
Willesden,
N.W.10.
July 5th, 19—.

Dear Mrs. Fitch,

Thanks for your letter regarding accommodation for myself and family. I am writing to accept your terms of — pounds per week, including cooking, attendance and all the usual extras.

In a few days I shall write telling you at what time on July 15th we shall arive, and I shall then include a list of the supplies we shall require at the outset.

We intend to stay for a fortnight.

Yours sincerely,
Rose Woodfield.

Letter Thanking Somebody for Being " Taken Out "
(By a Youngster)

> 38, Cantrell Avenue,
> Sidford,
> Surrey.
>
> July 8th, 19—.

Dear Uncle Bob,

I am writing to tell you how much I enjoyed myself the day before yesterday.   You gave me a really fine time and I think I was very lucky.

What I liked most was...;

but it was grand to have dinner (tea) with you in a super restaurant.   In fact, every moment of the time was good.

> So thank you very much.
> Your affectionate nephew,
> Phillip.

(Nephews and nieces should understand that uncles and aunts are very appreciative of letters of thanks.)

Letter Thanking Someone for Being " Taken Out "
(By an Adult)

> 38, Cantrell Avenue,
> Sidford,
> Surrey.
>
> May 16th, 19—.

Dear Mrs. Leverson,

Just a line to tell you how much I enjoyed last Tuesday evening and to thank you for taking me to the ....
....

For a long time I have wanted to see it (or go there) and now I feel I have achieved one of my ambitions.

I never was a great one for going to things by myself and I appreciated your company very much.

It was a really enjoyable evening.

Yours sincerely,

Joan Boardman.

Letter Expressing Thanks for a Christmas Present (By a Youngster)

539, Ellerton Drive,
Leeds.

27—12—37.

Dear Mrs. Catchpool,

I had a nice lot of Christmas presents—mechanical toys, several books, a paint box, and your chemical set. How did you know that I wanted such a set ? It was just the very thing that I had longed for, as nearly all my friends at school have them. I have made up a lot of chemicals with it already.

I hope Bernard had a nice lot of presents and that he enjoyed Christmas as much as I did.

Yours sincerely,

Michael.

Letter Asking a Friend for Permission to Make him Executor of a Will

54, Blackhorse Avenue,
Cottenham,
Cambs.

July 8th, 19—.

Dear Mr. Wallis,

I want to ask a favour and I sincerely hope you will see your way to granting it.

I am about to make my will and know of nobody who would perform the part of Executor more conscientiously than you would. Therefore, may I fill in your name as Executor on my will ?

I know it is a thankless task, but if you said yes it would go a long way towards setting my mind at rest.

Yours sincerely,
S. Watson.

(An executor should, properly, be someone who has every expectation of being alive and active when the person who makes the will dies.)

Letter Requesting a Free Sample of Some Advertised Goods

8, Birchfield Drive,
Actonbury,
Dorset.

May 18th, 19—.

Samfum, Ltd.,
Dept. D.M.15,
Queen Mary's Rd.,
N.W.16.

Dear Sirs,

Please send me a free sample of Samfum. A postage stamp is enclosed.

Yours faithfully,
Amy Chatterton.

(You need not trouble to mention in your letter in what paper you saw the advertisement. The firm will know without you telling them, as they have " keyed " their address. The letters in " Dept. D.M. 15." stand for the initials of the newspaper and the figures, the number of the advertisement. Thus, you read the offer in the 15th advertisement that Samfum put in " The Daily Magnet.")

Letter to a Store Advertising Goods for Sale

634, Crescent Road,
Ambleford,
Hants.

June 18th, 19—.

Messrs. Berry's, Ltd.,
Bargain Dept.

Dear Sirs,

In to-day's " Daily Express," you advertise overalls at £5.50.

Please send me two of them, one blue and one green, both in:

46 in. length.

Enclosed is my cheque for £12 to include the cost of postage.

Yours faithfully,
Annie Turnbury.

(If the advertisement gives a serial numbering to the goods, be careful to quote it, as it will help to avoid mistakes. Always cross a cheque sent through the post.)

Letter to a Mail-Order House Regarding the Purchase of Goods

854, Hamfrith Road,
Liverpool.

April 3rd, 19—.

Messrs. Lockie & Samson, Ltd.

Dear Sirs,

In to-day's " Daily Gazette " you have an adver tisement offering an extra heavy-quality wire Vegetable Rack at £5.50 plus £1 postage.

Please send me one of them.   My P.O. for £6.50 is enclosed.

Yours faithfully,
Frances Redwood.

(It helps the firm, if you mention the name of the newspaper

in which you saw the article advertised. Never send a postal order through the post without crossing it, and it is advisable to write the name of the firm on the line supplied for the purpose.)

Letter to a Mail-Order House Regarding the Purchase of Goods

854, Hamfrith Rd.,
Liverpool.
April 3rd, 19—.

Messrs. Lockie & Samson, Ltd.
Dear Sirs,
Please forward to me at the above address, C.O.D., the following items advertised in this morning's " Daily Gazette."

3 pairs Ladies' Stockings, size 10 tan, at 50p per pair	£1.50
6 Handkerchiefs, with initial R, ladies' size	£1.50
1 Double Bed Spread, No. 7 . .	£20.00
Total Cost . . .	£23.00

Yours faithfully,
Frances Redwood.

(*Keep such a letter as brief as possible ; but do not omit to give all the necessary particulars. Tabulate the items as here, whenever practicable.*)

Letter to the Editor of a Newspaper, for Publication, referring to a Matter of Public Interest

14, Falcon Road,
Merton Rd., S.W.19.
March 10th, 19—.

The Editor,
" The Daily Gazette."
Dear Sir,
This afternoon, I recorded my vote in the Parlia-

mentary Election and I am disgusted to find that voting by ballot does not carry with it the secrecy which Englishmen cherish.

Every ballot paper bore a serial number and, on the back of the counterfoil, the clerk wrote the voter's registration number.

It is thus a possibility that an official might compare a " filled in " voting paper with the figures on a counterfoil and, in this way, discover how Mr. or Mrs. So-and-so voted.

The practice needs the earnest consideration of the fair-minded and free-loving people of the country.

Yours faithfully,
Charles Wilson.

VI

BUSINESS MATTERS

See also the sections on " Situations, Appointments," and " Circular Advertising Letters."

In those specimens where the date and sender's address are omitted, it is assumed that such letters would be typewritten on a firm's headed notepaper, when they would naturally be dated in the ordinary course of business routine.

Letter from an Employee Asking for an Increased Salary

> 27, Kingsbridge Mansions,
> Putney,
> S.W.15.
> October 28th, 19—.

R. Fullerton Esq.,
Messrs. Fullerton & Sons, Ltd.

Dear Sir,

I am writing to ask if you could consider the question of my salary.

During the last two years I have not had an increase, though think you will agree that many responsibilities have been added to my work during this period.

I am very happy in the office and like my work, but with a growing family at home and an ever-increasing expenditure, in consequence, I find it difficult to balance my budget.

An addition to my salary would make all the difference.

> Yours faithfully,
> G. S. Blackman.

Letter Offering Goods at Special Prices

S. Bannister Esq.

Dear Sir,

We have recently purchased, at fairly advantageous prices, large stocks of —— and ——. Knowing that you are interested in these, we have pleasure in informing you that we are offering them at the following low prices :

. . . .

. . . .

. . . .

We are selling these rapidly, and as we cannot possibly repeat the offer, we respectfully suggest that it will be to your advantage to inform us of your requirements at an early date.

> We are, Sir,
> Yours faithfully,
> Wormald, Roberts & Co., Ltd.

Letter Sent with a Catalogue of Prices by a Business House

G. Loveday Esq.

Dear Sir,

We have much pleasure in forwarding our Priced Catalogue for the current year. We venture to suggest that it will be worth your while to glance through it, and would especially direct your attention to Sections C and D.

In opening new Departments for the sale of these goods, we have made it our aim, by means of efficient organisation and careful extensive buying, to offer goods of the first quality at moderate prices. A comparison of our prices with the average of the market will, we think, prove that we have achieved some measure of success in this.

Our stocks of all goods are larger and more varied than

ever, and we shall be happy to send you samples of any particular lines in which you are interested.

We should greatly appreciate a personal visit, if you can spare the time.

> We are, Sir,
> > Yours faithfully,
> > > Smith, Sons, and Co. Ltd.

Letter of Enquiry about the Price of Goods

> 769, Burdett Road,
> Bristol.
> > March 8th, 19—.

Messrs. John Mathers & Son.

Dear Sirs,

I am informed that you are manufacturers of ——. If this is the case, will you please let me know if you can supply me with the undermentioned, and quote your best trade terms ?

. . . . — — . . . .
. . . . — — . . . .

Delivery will be required (f.o.r.) within two months of date of order.

> Yours faithfully,
> George Brown.

Letter in Reply to the Previous Example

G. Brown Esq.

Dear Sir,

In reply to your enquiry of 8th March, we have much pleasure in submitting to you the following quotation :

. . . .
. . . .

We are prepared to allow you 10 per cent. discount as

a retailer, and our terms are 5 per cent. for cash, monthly a/c.

A sample has been despatched to you under separate cover.

As the actual manufacturers, we are confident that you will find our quotation extremely favourable. Owing, however, to the uncertain state of the market, this offer remains open for fourteen days only.

Trusting to hear from you in due course,

We are, Sir,

Yours faithfully,

John Mathers and Son.

A Letter from a Business House Apologising for a Mistake

R. Tottenham Esq.

Dear Sir,

With reference to your letter of 9th March we deeply regret that, by an oversight, we omitted to credit you for goods returned on 10th February. An amended statement is enclosed herewith.

With reference to ——, we would respectfully point out that our offer of 6th February was for seven days only, and that your order was not placed until the 28th.

You will understand that, owing to the fluctuating state of the market, it is impossible for us to maintain a fixed price for goods such as ——.

Apologising for any inconvenience that may have been caused,

We remain,

Yours faithfully,

Arnold and Bighead.

Letter of Allotment of Shares Issued by a Company

M. Jones Esq.

Dear Sir,

In response to your application, we beg to inform you that the Directors are allotting you 50 shares in this Company.

The amount you have paid on application is £10.

The amount now due from you is £27.

Will you be good enough to pay this amount on or before Feb. 1st, 19— ?

The final instalment of 50p per share should be remitted on April 1st, 19—.

All payments should be made to the Company's Bankers The London and District Bank, Ltd., Burford.

By Order of the Board of Directors,

Jane Dyson

(Secretary).

Letter Calling up Unpaid Share Capital

B. F. Austen Esq.

Dear Sir,

I am instructed to give you notice that at a general meeting of the Directors and Shareholders of this Company, held at the above address on Oct. 31st, 19—, it was decided to make a call of 20p per share on the unpaid capital.

Will you, therefore, kindly send a cheque for £50 to the Company's Bankers, the Anglo-Foreign Bank, Ltd., 529, Bishopsgate, E.C. before December 1st ?

Yours faithfully,

Robert Fullerton

(Secretary).

Letter to Shareholders giving Notice of a Company's Annual Meeting

T. Timson Esq.

    Sir,

      Notice is hereby given that the Annual General Meeting of Bourne and Brown, Ltd. will be held at Exeter Hall, Basinghall Lane, E.C.1 on the fifteenth day of August next, at 2.30 p.m. to receive and consider the annual report, and to transact any other business which, under the Company's Articles of Association, ought to be transacted at this meeting.

F. A. Bourne
(Secretary).

    (The law requires that seven clear days' notice must be given to shareholders of all meetings.)

Letter Used by a Company When Paying a Dividend

T. Timson Esq.

    Dear Sir,

      I beg to hand you herewith a warrant in respect of the dividend for the half year ending August 31st, 19—, upon the shares standing in your name in the books of the Company, as follows :

    Dividend on — *Preference Shares of £1 each

      at the rate of 6% per annum   .   .   ·£———

    Less Income Tax at —— in the £ .   .   ·£———

    Net Amount   .   .   .   .   .   ·£———

    I hereby certify that the amount stated hereon has been deducted for Income Tax and will be paid by me to the proper Officer for the Receipt of Taxes.

Yours faithfully,
F. A. Bourne
(Secretary).

    *(*Or whatever kind of shares are concerned.)*

Letter Explaining Absence from a Meeting

> 74, Holmwood Drive,
> Wandsworth,
> S.W.18.
>
> January 14th, 19—.

Dear Mr. Appleton,

I very much regret to have to tell you that it will be impossible for me to attend the annual meeting of Bankside and Brown to-morrow afternoon.

I have been in bed a week with lumbago and only got up to-day for the first time. The doctor tells me that I must not go out for some days yet. Thus, you see, it is hopeless for me to think of being present to-morrow afternoon.

May I ask you to convey my apologies to the Chairman and to the members generally ?

> Yours sincerely,
> S. Millward.

Letter Apologising for not being able to keep a Business Appointment

> 51, Goldheron Rd.,
> Shepherd's Bush,
> June 30th, 19—.

B. Martin Esq.

Dear Sir,

Since my letter to you of 24th June, certain circumstances have arisen which will compel my absence from town during the next ten days ; consequently, I shall be unable to call on you as promised on 1st July.

I am sorry thus to postpone our conference, but I trust you will excuse me. After the 6th July, I shall be entirely at your disposal, and will call on you at your convenience, if you will kindly notify me of the date and time.

> Yours faithfully,
> L. Seers.

A Short Letter of Acknowledgment

Glaslyn,
Cumberland Drive,
Beechford.

8 :3 : 37

Messrs. Wilcox & Jones, Ltd.

Dear Sirs,

I beg to acknowledge the recept of your letter of 4th March, and to say that it shall have my careful attention.

I hope to give you a definite answer within the next day or two.

Yours faithfully,
R. Goodyear.

Letter from a Firm Apologising to a Customer for Delay in Supplying Goods

E. Fyfield Esq.

Dear Sir,

We much regret that we have been unable to complete your order by the fifteenth, as promised.

Unfortunately, we have experienced considerable difficulty in obtaining raw materials, owing to ——. The position has now, however, improved a little, and we are making every effort to deliver the goods with the least possible delay.

A consignment of —— or more will be forwarded to you to-morrow, certain ; and the balance we anticipate will be finished by June 10th at the latest.

As the circumstances have been altogether beyond our control, we hope you will accept this explanation and arrangement, and will continue to favour us with your orders.

We are, Sir,
Yours faithfully,
M. Taylor, Ltd.

Letter from a Shopkeeper Apologising to a Customer for not being able to Supply Goods Ordered

Mrs. Cutler.

Dear Madam,

With reference to your letter of the 12th July, and our reply thereto, we regret to inform you that we now find it impossible to obtain the articles you require within the time specified. Those firms which we believed to be manufacturers of these articles inform us that they are no longer made in this country. Please accept our apologies for misinforming you.

We may add that while the specimens enclosed are not exactly the same as your sample, we think they may be near enough to suit your needs. We can supply them at —— and can deliver immediately.

Assuring you of our best attention,

Yours faithfully,

Butler Bros.

Letter Accompanying MS. to an Editor

15, Heathman's Crescent,
Hampden,
Warwickshire.

The Editor,   Oct. 8th, 19—
" The Star Magazine."

Dear Sir,

I have pleasure in submitting to you a short story entitled ——, hoping that you may find it suitable for publication.

The MS. contains about 5,000 words.

Yours faithfully,

Jean Allison.

(*Keep this covering letter as short as possible and enclose a stamped addressed envelope of suitable size for the return of your MS. if not accepted.*)

VII

CLUBS, SOCIETIES, ETC.

Letter Notifying a Member that His or Her Club Subscription Is Due

> The Castleways,
> Shirley upon Avon,
> Gloucestershire.
> April 1st, 19—.

Miss N. Harker.

Dear Madam,

As secretary of the Castleways Tennis Club, I have to inform you that the annual subscription of twenty pounds to the Club is now due.

I shall be pleased to receive your cheque within the next few days.

> Yours faithfully,
> Catherine Burke.

Letter Requesting Payment of an Overdue Subscription to a Club

> The Castleways,
> Shirley upon Avon,
> Gloucestershire.
> June 15th, 19—.

Miss N. Harker.

Dear Madam,

Please forgive my mentioning it, but your subscription

to the Castleways Tennis Club is overdue.   There is a rule which says it should be paid before April 30th, in each year.   Could you see to the matter, as soon as possible?   The subscription is twenty pounds.   Hoping that you will have a very enjoyable tennis season,

> Yours faithfully,
>> Catherine Burke.

(This letter presumes that the writer and receiver are acquainted.   If they were friends it would have been addressed to " Dear Miss Harker " and terminated with " Yours sincerely.")

Letter Requesting Payment of an Overdue Subscription to a Club

> The Three Turrets,
> Borsfield, Kent.
>> Aug. 1st, 19—.

My dear Molly,
    It's that sub. of yours that I want.   Here we are in August and your cheque for the Victoria Tennis Club subscription has not reached me yet!   By Rule 7, any member who hasn't paid up months ago is liable to be shot at dawn, so you see what the fates have in store for you.

Now, Molly, joking apart, send along your sub. like a dear, and help me to get my books straight.   Do it to-night, before you forget.

> Yours sincerely,
>> Madge.

(It often pays better to write a joking type of letter than one of legal form, in a case of this kind.   Of course, the writer must be on very friendly terms with the recipient, or the wording will be in bad taste.)

Letter Requesting Payment of an Overdue Subscription to a Club

The Three Turrets,
Borsfield, Kent.
August 10th, 19—

Miss R. Plunkett.
Dear Madam,

I regret to note that your subscription to the Victoria Tennis Club is still outstanding. By the Club's Rules (No. 7), all subscriptions are due on Jan. 1st, of each year and no member is allowed to play on the courts after August 1st, if her subscription is still unpaid.

In the circumstances, I should be glad if you could forward to me your subscription (twenty pounds) by return.

Yours faithfully,
M. Jessop.

(This is a suitable letter to use when previous letters of request have been sent and the writer still does not wish to be too firm.)

Letter Requesting Payment of an Overdue Subscription to a Club

The Three Turrets,
Borsfield, Kent.
Aug. 30th, 19—

Miss R. Plunkett.
Dear Madam,

My Committee request me to inform you that, by Rule 7 of the Victoria Tennis Club, no member whose subscription is outstanding on August 1st, for the current year, may play on the courts.

As your subscription has not been received, I am

directed to say that the Committee will be compelled, reluctantly, to enforce the rule in your case.

>Yours faithfully,
>M. Jessop.

(*A letter to be used as a last resort.*)

Letter Referring to the Formation of a Local Society

>The Homestead,
>Ditchford.
>March 2nd, 19—.

Miss Harley.

Dear Madam,

At an informal meeting held here last evening, it was decided to consider the advisability of instituting a local literary and debating society.

It was proposed to hold an open meeting to discuss the matter at the Lopping Hall, next Wednesday, at 7.15 p.m.

Knowing that you are interested in local affairs of this nature, I am venturing to ask if we may have the pleasure of your attendance ?

The need for such a society, we believe, is great and many residents will, we hope, avail themselves of the social intercourse which it will afford them.

>Yours very truly,
>S. Blandford.

Letter in Reply to a Request from a Person who Wishes to Become a Member of a Club

>Four Winds Golf Club,
>Hatherway,
>Sussex.
>July 1st, 19—

Dr. A. Grant.

Dear Sir,

I am directed to inform you that, at a meeting of the Four Winds Golf Club, held in the Club House, last evening, your name was submitted to the Members.

I am pleased to report that you were unanimously elected a member of the Club.

I enclose forms 3 and 4, which I shall be glad for you to complete and return to me, at your convenience.

Yours faithfully,
A. Z. Bowley,
Secretary.

Letter Notifying a Society Meeting

Oakdene,
Pershore Rd.,
Stamford.

E. Turner Esq.   Nov. 8th, 19—.

Dear Sir,

I beg to inform you that the next meeting of the Pershore–Stamford Debating Society will be held in the Parish Rooms on Thursday, Nov. 26th, at 7.45 p.m.

Miss Cathcart will open the meeting with a debate on "That this Society Views with Alarm the Increasing Folly of Nations." The opposer is Mr. Learoyd. The subject will be opened for debate when the speakers have concluded.

Yours faithfully,
Stanley Archer.

Letter Asking for a Club Fixture

THE MOUNTFORD CRICKET CLUB
Secretary—J. B. Pearce
Elmfields,
Hackbury,
Berks.

The Secretary,   March 1st, 19—.

All Saints' Cricket Club.

Dear Sir,

The Committee of the Mountford Cricket Club has instructed me to approach you with a view to arranging, if possible, a match with the All Saints' Cricket Club.

I need hardly say that we should be extremely pleased, if it were possible.

Our Vacant Dates are.............................

We play on Elmfields Green and our dressing rooms are..

We usually commence at ....   (time).

Hoping for a favourable reply,

Yours sincerely,

J. B. Pearce.

Letter Asking for a Club Fixture

123, Adelaide Rd.,

Chatsworth,

Gloucester.

July 16th, 19—.

The Secretary,

The United Rangers F.C.

Dear Sir,

We are now drawing up our fixture list for the coming season and are anxious to meet the United Rangers.

We usually play two elevens every Saturday, one at home and the other away.

The dates which we still have vacant are :

....

....

....

If any of these dates are convenient to your club, we shall be pleased to book them for both your first and second elevens. We do not mind which team plays on your ground and which on ours.

Hoping that we shall be able to meet,

Yours sincerely,

A. S. Potter

(Secretary to the Chatsworth Rovers).

(*Arrange the vacant dates in column form so that they may be easily noted.*)

Letter Asking for a Club Fixture

39, Spearholme Rd.,
Southgates,
Hull.

3rd Sept. 19—.

The Secretary,
Southgates United Football Club.

Dear Sir,

I am instructed to ask if it would be possible for your Club to arrange a match with us, the Meadow Green Football Club.

We have the following dates still open :

> Saturday, Oct. — at home.
> Saturday, Nov. — away.
> Saturday, Jan. — at home.
> Saturday, Feb. — at home.

If any of these dates are suitable, we should be happy to meet your First Team.

Hoping for a favourable reply,

Yours sincerely,
A. B. Jones.
(Secretary.)

Letter Asking for a Club Fixture

THE MAYFIELD TENNIS CLUB
Secretary, A. S. Goode,

395, Mortlock Rd.,
Stainton.

April 3rd, 19—.

The Secretary,
The Argyll Tennis Club.

Dear Sir,

Our Club is very anxious to arrange a friendly match with the Argyll Tennis Club, if such is possible.

In the first instance, we would like to suggest a Saturday

early in July, but other dates could be fixed, if preferred.

We could make up a tournament of mixed doubles or singles, whichever you wished.

Hoping that something may be arranged,

Yours sincerely,

A. S. Goode.

Letter Replying to a Club Asking for a Fixture

Under the Elms,

Porsham,

Gloucester.

July 30th, 19—.

Dear Mr. Potter.

In reply to your request for a fixture with our club, I wish to say that we shall be pleased to play you on Saturday, Jan. — ; kick off at 2.15 p.m.

We have booked your first eleven to play here and, if you are agreeable, for our second eleven to visit your ground.

Yours sincerely,

F. Halsey.

(Secretary to The United Rangers F.C.)

(Those who have had experience with the arranging of club fixtures know that many unnecessary letters have to be written because Secretaries fail to supply adequate particulars. The date, the time, which eleven will be visiting, and the location of the ground, if difficult to find, should all be given.)

Letter Relating to the Annual Meeting of a Society

16, Blackford Rd.,

Glasgow, S.7.

July 8th, 19—.

Miss E. Ward.

Dear Madam,

I beg to inform you that the annual meeting of the

Blackford Debating Society will be held on July 30th.

The Committee earnestly hope that it will be convenient for you to attend.

Motions must be submitted in writing to me by July 1st, if they are to be printed on the agenda.

Yours faithfully,
Agnes Hirchfield.

Place—Central Hall, Blackford Rd.
Time—8.15 p.m.

Letter to a Secretary Requesting him to Include a Motion on the Agenda of the Next Meeting

39, Atlantic Row.
Newford.
August 19th, 19—.

R. Temple Esq.

Dear Sir,

I am in receipt of your letter, advising me that the next meeting of the Newford Debating Society is to be held on Sept. 1st.

Will you please allow me to submit the following motion, for inclusion on the agenda ?

" That in future, members who are in arrears with their subscriptions shall be denied the right of voting on matters affecting the policy of this Society."

Yours faithfully,
F. K. Chesterfield.

VIII

ILLNESS, DEATH, ETC.

Letters touching on the questions which arise in the case of illness or death are given in this section.

Letter of Sympathy and Offer of Help in a Case of Illness

> 67, Churtwood Rd.,
> Anerley,
> S.E.20.
> March 18th, 19—.

Dear Harry,

We are all so sorry to hear that Mary is very ill and I need not tell you that we are deeply sympathetic.

As you have both been so good to us in the past, we do hope that you will allow us to help you, if we can be of any assistance.

Jane* is worrying over your two youngsters and wondering how you are managing with them. She suggests that they come here and that she looks after them. As you know, she would be a second mother to them. Would you like her to fetch them, so that you would have more time to devote to Mary?

If there is anything we can do, do please make use of us. And, Harry, we are thinking of you and hoping for better news.

> Yours sincerely,
> John.

The writer's wife.

Letter of Sympathy and Offer of Help in a Case of Illness

54, Bowden Lane,
Charlton,
S.E.7.
Feb. 8th, 19—.

Dear Mrs. Rogers,

We are extremely sorry to hear that Mr. Rogers is very ill, and we do hope that you will soon have some better news to report.

Is there any way in which we can be of some slight assistance ? On such occasions one is often hard put to be able to manage ; but if there is anything we can do, please do not hesitate to let us know.

Would you care for Teddy to come here for a few days, as he is so young and must be taking up a great deal of your time ? He would be quite happy with Kenneth.

With every sympathy,

Yours sincerely,
Myra Dolling.

Letter of Sympathy Regarding Someone who is Ill

39, Fircroft Road,
Blackheath,
S.E.3.
January 26th, 19—.

Dear Mr. Gregory,

I am extremely sorry to hear of Mrs. Gregory's illness, and I do hope that she will soon be much better.

It must be an anxious time for you and you have my fullest sympathy.

Let us hope that, in a short while, you will have some better news.

> With kind regards,
> > Yours sincerely,
> > > Edgar Billing.

(Do not use this letter if it is known that the invalid is not likely to recover.)

Letter of Sympathy Regarding Someone who is Ill

> 39, Fircroft Road,
> > Blackheath,
> > > S.E.3.
> > > > January 26th, 19—.

Dear Mr. Gregory,

I have heard that Mrs. Gregory is very ill and I am writing to say how sorry I am.

You must be dreadfully worried ; but perhaps you will be able to gain some slight consolation from the knowledge that many of your friends are feeling for you.

My wife joins with me in sympathy.

> > Yours sincerely,
> > > Edgar Billing.

(Suitable in extreme cases when the invalid is not likely to recover.)

Letter of Sympathy to an Invalid

> 39, Fircroft Rd.,
> > Blackheath,
> > > S.E.3.
> > > > Jan. 26th, 19—.

Dear Mrs. Gregory,

We are extremely sorry to hear you are ill, and we do hope and trust you will soon be better.

We are thinking of you every day and wondering how you are.

If there is anything we can do, please do not fail to make use of us.   We shall 'phone, from time to time, to learn how you are progressing.

> With kindest regards,
> Yours sincerely,
> **Ada Billing.**

Letter Written by a Daughter for Her Sick Mother

> Lewington Grange,
> Lewington,
> Cheshire.
> December 5th, 19—.

Dear Mrs. Axford,

It is very good of you to write such a cheery letter to Mother, and the flowers you sent delighted her.

I am sorry to say she is still in bed and very ill.   The doctor comes every day, and sometimes he has been twice.   I am afraid it is going to be a long and weary business.

The only bright feature is Mother's pluck.   She threatens to be out of bed and up within a week, which is, of course, an impossibility.

When she is a little better, she would enjoy a visit from you ; but at present, the doctor will not allow her to see anybody.

> Yours sincerely,
> **Flora Perry.**

Letter to a Friend in Hospital

> Avondale,
> Hampstead Drive,
> N.W.2.
> January 5th, 19—.

Dear Arnold,

I was mighty surprised to hear yesterday that you were in hospital, and have had to have an operation,

I'm sorry that fate has been so unkind to you, and I trust that it will not be long before you are back at home.

I don't know much about hospitals, but if anyone can find them amusing, I am sure you would be just the one to do so.

You have always had a facility for seeing the funny side of a situation, and I guess you'll do it this time.

If I may come in and see you sometime or other, it would be a pleasure to do so.

Best of luck,

Yours ever,

Derek.

Letter of Thanks for Sending Flowers to an Invalid

Ward 3,

The Cottage Hospital,

Dunham.

3—5—37.

Dear Mrs. Fletcher,

Now that I am able to sit up a little, I should like to thank you for the lovely flowers you sent in the other day. They are still as dainty and fresh as ever.

It was good of you to think of me and I appreciate your kindness.

Fortunately, I am improving, but it is a tedious business. Still, I must not grumble, as the change is in the right direction.

Yours sincerely,

Julia Troutbeck.

Letter to Neighbour about Invalid

Croftholme,

Taplow.

May 8th, 19—.

Dear Mrs. Jones,

I should take it as a favour if you would ask your

children to keep as quiet as possible for the next few days, as my husband is very ill. I know it is hard upon your youngsters, but the doctor says that perfect quiet is essential for his recovery.

Thanking you in anticipation, and with good wishes.

Yours sincerely,

Anne Marsh.

Letter to a Neighbour who is Ill

19, Trehurst Crescent,
Buxton.
Nov. 6th, 19—.

Dear Mrs. Mackay,

I have only just heard that you are laid up and under the care of the doctor. I am so sorry I do not know you more intimately, but if you will overlook that, I should be so very pleased to help you in any way I can.

May I come in and sit with you this afternoon? It would release your nurse, and be a change for yourself. I might then find out other ways in which I could be useful to you while you are ill.

Hoping you will soon pull round again,

Yours sincerely,

Martha Brown.

(*Such a letter as this would naturally be sent by hand.*)

Letter in Reply to the Previous Example

17, Trehurst Crescent,
Buxton.
Nov. 6th, 19—.

Dear Mrs. Brown,

It is so very kind of you to suggest coming in this afternoon to sit with me, and I shall be only too glad to see you if you will come about three o'clock. I am afraid it is my fault that we have not been better neighbours, but I do not readily make friends.

You will, I know, excuse a pencil note, but I am confined to bed.

Looking forward to seeing you,

Yours sincerely,
Agnes Mackay.

A Letter of Condolence

Hilltop Manor,
Upford.
January 21st, 19—.

My dear Mrs. Anderson,

I have just heard of your terrible loss and hasten to offer you my deepest sympathy. At such a time, it seems vain to try to express one's feelings : they are too overwhelming. But you may derive some tiny grain of comfort in knowing that there are friends near you who can share your sorrows. Believe me, all of us at the Manor are deeply grieved.

It does seem that the world is a heartless place, but now that it is all over, there should be some small ray of comfort in knowing that Henry is free from pain and suffering.

Please forgive this letter : it expresses my sorrow very poorly. I mean far more than I can write.

Yours very sincerely,
Marie Queensford.

Letter of Condolence on the Death of a Husband

Jersingham Hall,
Whichminster.
April 5th, 19—.

My dear Alice,

Were it not that I hope you look upon me as a very

real friend, I should hardly dare to intrude upon you now, even to assure you of my most heartfelt sympathy. May I tell you how deeply I am feeling with you and for you, though I know truly " The heart knoweth his own bitterness," and that there seems, perhaps, little or no ray of light on any side. I know that, too, so well. I will say no more, but only assure you again of my love and sympathy and my prayers for you.   Can I do anything for you in any way ?   You have only to let me know what it is.

All Whichminster feel that they have lost a real friend.

Yours very sincerely,
Effie Sternhold.

Letter of Condolence on a Death

39, Fircroft Road,
Blackheath,
S.E.3.
February 8th, 19—.

Dear Mr. Gregory,

I have just heard of the sad death of Mrs. Gregory, and Myra joins with me in saying how deeply sorry we are.

I am afraid I cannot tell you how much I feel about it all, but I know you will realise that it has come to us as a great shock.

We both had a great admiration for Mrs. Gregory, and we hope you will find some slight consolation in the knowledge that we are grieving at her loss.

In deepest sympathy,
Yours sincerely,
Edgar Billing.

Letter of Condolence on the Death of a Sister

Bywater Lodge,
Ousedale,
Yorks.

July 23rd, 19—.

My dearest Agnes,

I cannot tell you how deeply grieved I am about your sister. I knew Molly was very ill, of course, and was hoping to get over to see you both, but I did not realise that the end could possibly come like this, and so soon. I know what a terrible loss it will be to you, and what it will mean ; she was such a dear, dear girl. I always felt she was so good, and so thoughtful for others. There will be many who will miss her besides her own family. You will let me know, won't you, if there is anything that I can do for you ? With much love,

Yours very sincerely,

Diana.

Letter Informing a Friend or Relation of a Death

69, Fursewood Gardens,
Lincoln.

May 10th, 19—.

Dear Aunt Laura,

I am sure you will be very sorry to hear that Mother died last night. The end was peaceful.

I shall write to you later, when we know the arrangements.

Yours with love,

Myrtle.

(As, presumably, the occasion is one when many people will have to be informed, it is not expected that the letter will be other than very brief and to the point.)

Letter Replying to an Intimation of Death
From a Friend or Relative

> 798, Drury Lane,
> Lincoln.
> May 11th, 19—.

Dearest Myrtle,

I am most grieved to hear of your mother's death and do hope you are bearing up in the sad circumstances.

It must be a great comfort to you to be able to feel that you were always so good and considerate to your mother.   You   certainly   need   not   have   any   re-proaches.

I intend coming over to see you to-morrow (May 12th). I am so sorry, dear.

> Yours with love,
> **Aunt Laura.**

Letter Excusing Absence from Work on Account of
a Relative's Death

> 315, Hilltop Rd.,
> Hamberton,
> Shropshire.
> Nov. 8th, 19—.

F. Gilderson **Esq.**

Dear Sir,

I am very sorry to say that my father died yesterday. In the circumstances, it will not be possible for me to come to the office for a day or two.

Trusting that you will excuse my absence and apologising for the inconvenience I am causing,

> Yours faithfully,
> Adela Cunningham.

Letter Replying to an Intimation of Death From an Employer

3, The Market Square,
Hamberton,
Shropshire.

Nov. 9th, 19—

Dear Miss Cunningham,

I am very grieved to hear of your father's death. All your friends at the office wish me to convey their sincere condolences.

Please do not worry about coming back here. No doubt your mother needs your comfort. We shall not expect you for several days.

In sympathy,
Yours sincerely,
F. Gilderson.

Letter Notifying the Time of a Funeral

73, Westingford St.,
N.W.8.

H. Young Esq.   January 8th, 19—.

Dear Sir,

I have been asked by Miss Yeoman to inform you that the funeral of her father will take place on Tuesday, January 11th, at Holy Trinity Church, Exford St.. N.W.8, at 11.30 a.m.

Yours truly,,
S. Gosling.

Letter Informing an Executor of a Death

3, Jedburgh Road,
Richmond,
Surrey.

April 3rd, 19—.

Dear Mr. Pinckney,

I am sure you will be sorry to hear that my father died

last night. He was in his usual health until about a week ago, when he suddenly became ill.

I see from his papers that he had appointed you as one of the Executors of his will.

Yours sincerely,
Madge Ellam.

(Such a letter presumes that the writer is only slightly acquainted with the person to whom she is writing. Her main reason for sending the letter is to acquaint the Executor that he must enter on his duties forthwith.)

Formal Letter of Thanks for Sympathies, following a Death

69, Truscott Avenue,
Burlington,
Wolverhampton.

Mr. and Mrs. Ackroyd and Family gratefully acknowledge your very kind expression of sympathy in their sad loss, and they desire to thank you.

(Such a letter is usually printed. It is sent to all who wrote or visited personally, and, also, to those who sent wreaths.)

IX

LANDLORD AND TENANT

Letter from a Landlord to a Tenant, Reminding him that the Rent is Due

6, High St.,
Broadham, Sussex.
Dec. 28th, 19—.

R. Cuthbert Esq.
    Dear Sir,
    I beg to remind you that the rent, due from you on Dec. 25th, in respect of the premises situated at 54, Archway St., has not yet been received.
    I shall be obliged if you will send me a cheque in settlement at your earliest convenience.
                        Yours faithfully,
                            John Stewart.

Letter from a Landlord to a Tenant, Requesting Overdue Rent

6, High St.,
Broadham, Sussex.
Feb. 1st, 19—

R. Cuthbert Esq.
    Dear Sir,
    I have to call your attention to the fact that the rent due from you for the quarter ending December 25th last, in respect of the premises occupied by you at 54, Archway St., has not yet been received.

I regret to have to inform you that unless a settlement is forthcoming without any further delay, I shall be compelled to take such steps as the law affords.

Yours faithfully,
John Stewart.

Letter from Landlord Serving Notice to Quit on a Tenant

6, High Street,
Broadham, Sussex.
May 10th, 19—.

R. Cuthbert Esq.
Dear Sir,

I beg to give you notice to quit and deliver up possession of the premises, No. 54, Archway St., Broadham, which you hold of me, on the 29th day of September next.

Yours faithfully,
John Stewart.

Letter to a Landlord asking him to Effect Certain Repairs

60, Waldemar Avenue,
N.W.16.
June 29th, 19—

G. A. Blay Esq.
Dear Sir,

I regret to have to tell you that yesterday, the high winds loosened one of the chimney pots which crashed to the ground smashing a number of tiles.

I should be glad if you could see that the matter is put right as soon as possible, since every time it rains water runs through one of the ceilings.

Yours faithfully,
J. Sudbury.

Letter to a Landlord, as before, but Affecting Recurring Repairs

60, Waldemar Gardens,
N.W.16.
June 29th, 19—.

G. A. Blay Esq.
Dear Sir,

I am enclosing the rent for the quarter just ended, of the above premises.

I am sorry to say that many of the rooms are greatly in need of renovation. The sitting-room and the front bedroom are both in a bad state, and I must ask you to have them painted and papered.

Would you favour me by having these rooms seen to as soon as possible ?

Yours faithfully,
J. Sudbury.

Letter to a Landlord, Stronger in Tone than the Former

60, Waldemar Gardens,
N.W.16.
January 5th, 19—.

G. A. Blay Esq.
Dear Sir,

I am writing to call your attention to the necessity for repairing the —— at these premises. I do not wish to appear unduly persistent in the matter, but I would remind you that it is now nine months since I first called your attention to the defect.

Obviously, it is not to my advantage alone that the damaged parts be replaced, since the —— is affecting the surrounding walls.

Would you favour me with a reply within the next few days (as, failing a note from you, I shall be forced to acquaint the proper authorities) ?

Yours faithfully,

J. Sudbury.

(Only add the passage in brackets when it is really intended to take the step mentioned. In no case should the bracket-marks be used. They are merely given here to single out the passage in doubt.)

Letter from a Tenant Asking for a Reduction of Rent

5, Antill Gardens,
Brookhurst,
Essex.

Jan. 28th, 19—.

S. Ladberry Esq.

Dear Sir,

I am writing to ask if you will agree to a reduction of the rent I am paying for the above house ? I have lived here more than —— years and, during that time have never asked for an excessive amount of repairs, having done many small jobs myself.

The rent was fixed when vacant houses were few and wages were high. Since then, rents and wages have generally come down and I now find that I am paying more for this house than the sums paid by many of my neighbours.

As my own wages have shrunk, I feel bound to ask you to consider my request.

Yours faithfully,

S. A. Maidman.

Letter from a Landlord Refusing the Request of a Tenant to Reduce the Rent

61, Turnfield Lane,
Brookhurst,
Essex.

Feb. 1st, 19—.

S. A. Maidman Esq.

Dear Sir,

I am sorry to say that it is impossible to reduce the rent of the house of which you are the tenant.

The rent was fixed —— years ago, it is true ; but I then took into consideration that you were likely to be a good tenant, and put it at a very low figure.

Were I to make a reduction, there would be very little left for me after paying for repairs, meeting the taxes which are growing higher, and paying the ground rent.

In fact, I was wondering last quarter whether I ought not to raise the rent, owing to the rising taxes and other outgoings.

With regrets,
Yours faithfully,
S. Ladberry.

Letter from a Tenant Threatening to Leave if the Rent is not Reduced

5, Antill Gardens,
Brookhurst,
Essex.

Feb. 4th, 19—.

S. Ladberry Esq.

Dear Sir,

I am in receipt of your letter of Feb. 1st, in which you refuse to reduce the rent of this house.

I am sorry to say that, if this is your final decision, I shall be compelled to seek accommodation elsewhere.

My wages have been reduced —— times in the last —— years and the " cost of living " figures show that rents are coming down.

Close at hand, I find there are houses that suit my needs at lower rentals than mine.

In these circumstances, I must ask you to reconsider your decision, or I must move.

Yours faithfully,
S. A. Maidman.

Letter from a Landlord Raising the Rent of a Tenant

61, Turnfield Lane,
Brookhurst,
Essex.
March 3rd, 19——.

G. Lauriman Esq.

Dear Sir,

I am sending you formal notice that, as from June 25th, next, your rent will be increased from £— to £— per annum.

I am forced to take this step owing to the increase in rates.

I am, Dear Sir,
Yours faithfully,
S. Ladberry.

(Notices of this kind should be forwarded by registered letter, and the receipt preserved, in order to avoid any dispute as to delivery. The writer should make sure that he is giving the proper amount of notice if an agreement exists.)

Letter to a Tenant Refusing to do Repairs

43, Singleton Mews,
S.W.14.
January 19th, 19——.

G. Hunter Esq.

Dear Sir,

I am in receipt of your letter of January 18th, and regret to have to inform you that it is quite impossible to think of any repairs to the house for some time to come.

During the last two years the major part of the rent has been absorbed by renovations of one kind and another, and the property has been a severe drain on my own income.

From this I think you will see that, while I do not wish to be unreasonable, I am forced to refuse your request.

Yours faithfully,

A. Gifford.

Letter from a Landlord to an Outgoing Tenant asking the Latter to Allow a Prospective Tenant to See over the House

6, High Street,
Broadham,
Sussex.

Feb. 1st, 19—.

S. Davies Esq.

Dear Sir,

As your tenancy expires at the end of this quarter, may I ask if you could allow a prospective tenant to look over the house ?

It would be a gracious act on your part if you could favour me in this way.   Naturally, the person in question would only come by appointment and at a time entirely convenient to Mrs. Davies and yourself.

Yours faithfully,

John Stewart.

Letter from a Tenant asking for an Extension of Time to Pay the Rent

3, Seacome Villas,
Archery Fields,
Arden.

Feb. 7th, 19—.

M. Shawcross Esq.

Dear Sir,

I regret that you have had to write in connection with the rent, which is now overdue.

I am sorry to say that at the moment I am unable to meet your demand.   The last few months have proved a great strain on my finances, largely because ....
....

In all the circumstances, could I ask you to let the matter stand for a little while, and, during the interval, I will do my utmost to get the money together ?

Yours faithfully,
Peter A. Smithson.

(Fill in particulars, in the space left open, according to the personal conditions.)

Letter Asking Landlord to Wait for Payment of Rent

6, Amberley Villas,
Burchford,
Oxfordshire.
April 1st, 19—.

Dear Mr. Simpson,

I am exceedingly sorry to find that I must ask if you can possibly allow me to defer payment of rent due at Lady Day until the next quarter day, or I will, if possible, pay one-half of what is due at Lady Day in the middle of the ensuing quarter, and all that will then be due on Midsummer Day.   With my husband's long illness, and unexpectedly heavy school bills for the children at Christmas, I am really quite unable to find the rent this quarter.   I very much regret having to make this request, and shall be grateful to you if you will accept this arrangement.

Yours sincerely,
Gladys Jones.

(Mrs. Jones is asking a favour and, therefore, thinks it politic to write to Mr. Simpson as a friend, in order to alter the atmosphere from business to friendship.   That is why she forgoes the " Dear Sir " and the " Yours faithfully," that the circumstances really require.)

Letter Requesting the Half-Yearly Payment of Ground-Rent from the Tenant

> 6, High Street,
> Broadham, Sussex.
> Oct. 1st, 19—.

S. Finnemore Esq.

Dear Sir,

We beg to remind you that the Ground Rent respecting the undermentioned property became due last Quarter Day, and we shall be grateful if you will remit to us your cheque for the amount stated.

Will you please forward, for our perusal, the last receipt for the Fire Insurance premium regarding the property? We shall return it to you with the receipt for the Ground Rent.

> Yours truly,
> Steward and Darling.

Property—69, Archway St.
Period—Six Months ending Sep. 29.
Amount—
Less Income Tax—
Net—

Letter to Sanitary Authorities from a Tenant who Suspects Defects in the House he is Occupying

> 25, Moreton Street,
> Angleford.
> May 12th, 19—.

The Sanitary Inspector,
Angleford Town Hall.

Dear Sir,

I am the tenant at the above address and, for some considerable time have been uneasy about the sanitary

conditions here.   In particular, I find ....
I have written .... times to the landlord respecting
these matters and he refuses to take any notice.

In the circumstances, I consider it my duty to
inform you of what I believe are the conditions, in order
that your opinion may be obtained.

Yours faithfully,

Arthur Westlake.

*(Note—Before a tenant reports such a matter to the
authorities he should make sure that his agreement throws
the liability on the landlord and not on himself.)*

Letter Asking a Landlord to Release the Writer from the Tenancy before the Lease has Expired

308, Cumberland Rd.,

N.W.25.

Jan. 21st, 19—.

C. Potter Esq.

Dear Sir,

As my husband has just accepted the management of
some large works near to Bristol, we are anxious to move
down into that neighbourhood as soon as possible, but our
lease of this house has still, I know, three years to run.
Will you be so very kind as to consider this, and let us
know at your earliest convenience at what date, and on
what terms, you would be prepared to release us from the
remainder of our tenancy ?   We want, if possible, to get
away by Lady Day, and will, of course, be ready to
meet any reasonable terms you are kind enough to offer
us.   Regretting very sincerely that we find it necessary to
make this move, and with our kind regards,

Yours faithfully,

Mary Brookfield.

Letter from a House Owner to his Agent about Repairs

3, Cornfields,
Walmer,
Kent

July 3rd, 19—.

C. Rose Esq.

Dear Sir,

I hereby acknowledge receipt of rents for my houses Nos. 2, 4, 6, 8, in the Starwick Road for the quarter ending on June 24th, and am glad to note that these tenants are regular in their payments. I see that repairs are again required to the sink waste-pipe of No. 2, and to the kitchen ceiling and the roof of No. 4. On referring to my accounts with you, I find that the scullery sink at No. 2 was repaired only two months ago. Can you pull the tenants up about that, and suggest that there must surely have been careless usage on their part, or do you think the plumber was to blame? Will you kindly let me know what conclusion you come to? The work, must, of course, be done there, and to No. 4.

Yours faithfully,

G. Talbot.

(Do not omit to enclose the receipts, as stated.)

X

MONEY MATTERS

Letter Asking for a Bill to be Paid

E. Wolverton Esq.

Dear Sir,

A statement of our account was forwarded to you on August 10th. As we have not received a remittance, it has occurred to us that possibly our letter has been mislaid.

Will you kindly let us know whether this is the case, so that we may then supply a copy?

Yours faithfully,
Frank Acton & Co.

Letter Pressing for a Bill to be Paid

E. Wolverton Esq.

Dear Sir,

We much regret the necessity for calling attention once more to the account forwarded to you on ——. We have not pressed hitherto, as we concluded that the matter had escaped your notice owing, perhaps, to pressure of business.

Payment is now long overdue and we must ask that you will be good enough to make a settlement by return of post.

Yours faithfully,
Frank Acton & Co.

Letter Threatening Proceedings

> 50, Roman Terrace,
> Chalk Farm,
> N.W.1.
> July 16th, 19—.

A. Campion Esq.

Dear Sir,

Unless your account is settled within the next seven days, I shall be reluctantly obliged to place the matter in the hands of my solicitor.

> Yours faithfully,
> F. Putnam.

(It is important to note that a private person must not threaten proceedings in a definite way. Only a solicitor may do that. Any wording that suggests the writer is a solicitor, when he is not, may lead to serious trouble. Therefore, the proper course is to be vague, as in the example above.)

Letter Requesting the Repayment of a Loan

> 39, Grove Drive,
> Leicester.
> August 8th, 19—

Dear Mr. Angus,

Two or three months ago you were awkwardly placed over money matters and, at some inconvenience to myself, I lent you five pounds.

Now, it happens that I need the money which I handed to you. Will you therefore, please let me have the return of this sum ?

> Yours sincerely,
> S. Gurry.

(In such letters the aim should be not only to obtain the money but to retain the friendship.)

Letter Requesting the Repayment of a Loan (Drastic)

39, Grove Drive,
Leicester.

Sep. 8th, 19—.

Dear Mr. Angus,

A month has passed since I wrote to you asking for the return of the five pounds which I lent you two or three months previously.

As you have not troubled to reply, I take it that you only intend doing so under compulsion. I am, therefore, informing you that, unless the debt is paid before the end of the week, I am placing your letter and the receipt before my solicitor for him to deal with as he thinks fit.

Yours truly,

S. Gurry.

Letter Requesting a Settlement of an Account

M. Price Esq.

Dear Sir,

We shall be greatly obliged if you could favour us with a cheque for the goods supplied to you during October and November last.

Our accounts are balanced during the first week of January in each year, and the delay in receiving your settlement is preventing us from closing our ledgers.

A duplicate invoice is enclosed.

Yours faithfully,

pp. THE EASTWOOD STORES,
S. F. Fothergill.

A Stronger Letter Requesting a Settlement of an Account

M. Price Esq.

Dear Sir,

We regret to note that the account for goods supplied during October and November of last year is still outstanding.

We have already written to you several times regarding the matter and have furnished invoices, in duplicate.

In the circumstances, we regret to have to inform you that, unless we receive a settlement during the course of the week, we shall be obliged to instruct our solicitors to institute proceedings against you.

> Yours faithfully,
> pp. THE EASTWOOD STORES,
> S. F. Fothergill.

(*It is not wise to send such a letter unless proceedings are really intended.*)

Letter Replying to a Creditor who is Pressing for Payment

> 79, Redbridge Road,
> Axford,
> Herts.
> July 8th, 19—.

S. Jefferson Esq.

Dear Sir,

I have received your warning of legal proceedings with regard to our outstanding account, and I am sorry that you are inclined to push matters thus far at the present juncture.

You cannot desire a settlement more anxiously than I do myself ; but I feel it my duty to inform you that I cannot possibly pay at the present time. In a few weeks I am confident that I shall be able to do so, and I am prepared to accept a Bill at three months, if you care to draw one.

I sincerely regret the delay which has occurred, but trust that our relations may remain cordial.

> Yours faithfully,
> John Birch.

Letter Replying to a Creditor who is Pressing for Payment

79, Redbridge Rd.,
Axford,
Herts.

July 8th, 19—.

S. Jefferson Esq.

Dear Sir,

I was considerably surprised to receive this morning your letter threatening legal proceedings in the event of my not forwarding a full remittance within six days.

I deeply regret that you should consider such a step necessary. I would remind you that I have dealt with you for over two years, and that during that time I have settled monthly with promptitude.

Proceedings would put both of us to unnecessary trouble, without improving the position. As an old customer, I hope you will reconsider the matter, and be good enough to allow me a little grace.

I am forwarding a small remittance on account, as evidence of my good faith.

Thanking you for previous courtesy.

I am,
Yours faithfully,
John Birch.

Letter Requesting an Account to be Rendered

1, Victory Lane,
Chiswick.

May 15th, 19—.

Dear Dr. Taylor,

As I am moving from the district in a few days' time, I must ask if you could render your account to me, so that I may settle it before leaving.

At the same time, I should like to thank you for the care you have taken of my family and myself. It is with regret that we shall find your services no longer available.

Yours sincerely,

F. Carey.

Letter Requesting that a Statement of Account be Rendered

Alloa Road,
Newington,
Kent.

August 11th, 19—.

Messrs. Perkins & Lambton, Ltd.

Dear Sirs,

I should be obliged if you would forward to me, at an early date, your statement of account up to and including the 31st ult.

Yours faithfully,

S. Warwick.

(*Note that* ult. *is the short for* ultimo *and means* last. *Above, therefore, it means* last month. *The opposite to* ult. *is* prox., *the short for* proximo, *the meaning being* next. Inst. *means* present. *Thus, if in August a letter reads* 31st ult., *it refers to July* 31st ; *if it reads* 30th prox., *it refers to September* 30th, *and if it mentions* 31st inst. *it means August* 31st.)

Letter Pointing out an Error in a Statement Received

Alloa Rd.,
Newington,
Kent.

August 15th, 19—.

Messrs. Perkins & Lambton, Ltd.

Dear Sirs,

I have duly received your statement under yesterday's date. Before settling, however, I must point out that

Item 4, in respect of ——, does not agree with your quotation submitted to me on the 6th ult.   Further, you have omitted to credit me with the value of the goods returned on July 10th, for which I hold your carrier's receipt.

Upon receiving an amended statement, I will forward to you my cheque in full settlement.

Yours faithfully,
S. Warwick.

Letter Asking a Friend for a Loan of Money

7, Priory Grove,
Nightingale Lane,
Palmer's Green, N.
June 8th, 19—.

My dear Woodward,

I am extremely sorry to worry you on such a subject, but a serious operation on my wife has exhausted my small reserve fund and I am finding myself in difficulties at the moment.   If you could possibly let me have twenty or twenty-five pounds for three or four months, it would see me safely round the corner and relieve my mind of a great strain.   I have tried my brother William, but with his large family, he has no margin and cannot help me just now, when it is essential for Maud's recovery that she should be sent off to——.

Don't hesitate to say " no " if you really cannot do it—I am sure you will if you can.

Yours sincerely,
Jack Thompson.

Letter in Reply to the Previous Example

309, The Broadway,
Golder's Green, N.W.11.
June 10th, 19—.

My dear Jack,

What rough luck ! I'm extremely sorry for you and your plucky wife. As it happens, I can easily do what you ask and enclose a cheque for twenty-five pounds. Don't feel obliged to pay it back in three or four months, but give your wife every possible chance to regain her strength—twelve months hence will do quite well for me.

My kind regards to both of you,

Yours ever,

Hugh Woodward.

Another Letter In Reply to the Request for a Loan of Money

309, The Broad,

Golder's Green, N.W.

June 10th, 19—.

My dear Thompson,

I was extremely sorry to hear your bad news, especially as I cannot just now help you in the way you suggest. I am, however, sending two five-pound notes, all I can do for you at the moment.   I hope it will clear you of your most pressing difficulties and give you time to try some other friend.   Drop me a line if you fail elsewhere, and I will, if possible, let you have another ten pounds when I get my salary at the end of the month.

No hurry for repayment, and don't let your wife worry at all.

All good wishes,

Yours ever,

Hugh Woodward.

Letter Appealing for Charitable Funds

Haverfield,

Chesterfield,

Nottingham.

S. Grout Esq.   June 1st, 19 —

Dear Sir,

May I appeal to you, as one who has never failed to take a charitable interest in cases of local need, for a little financial help ?

As perhaps you know, I have been appointed honorary treasurer to the —— Fund. The work we are doing is of the utmost importance and the cases which come to our notice are indeed distressing.

In the past six months we have assisted some forty odd persons, all of whom would have been in dire circumstances had not charitable friends supplied us with funds.

At the moment we are in debt, and unless we can rely for help on you and other generous residents of the neighbourhood, we fear that the good work of the —— Fund must cease or, at the least, suffer curtailment.

May I appeal to you once more for help? The need is pressing.

Yours very truly,
Viola Carrington.

Letter Asking the Recipient to Assist a Deserving Case

Surridge Vicarage,
Merford, Bucks.
Nov. 2nd, 19—.

Mrs. Hailey.

Dear Madam,

Your friend Mrs. Roper has suggested that I write to you with regard to a very sad case which has come under my notice in the parish.

A Mrs. Kingsley has recently lost her husband in very touching circumstances. She has three children of school age and is entirely without support. Her husband was a good worker, but his long illness consumed what little money he was able to save.

Mrs. Roper thinks you might be able to offer Mrs. Kingsley some casual employment. She is a good cook, good at needlework and capable in many ways. If there

is anything you could give her to do, we should be extremely grateful.

Yours very truly,
Madge Blyfield.

Letter from a Firm which has Received an Order for Goods, but Requires a Reference or Remittance before sending the Goods

John Marchant Esq.
Dear Sir,

We wish to thank you for your order of November
11th and to inform you that it is being given our prompt
attention.

Since this is the first occasion on which we have had
business relations with you, we should deem it a favour if
you would supply us with your banker's reference or a
remittance.

Yours faithfully,
THE CHEAPSIDE TRADERS.
A. M. Woods.

Letter Complaining of Length of Credit taken by a Customer

Messrs. Abbott & Coles, Ltd.
Dear Sirs,

We note from our ledgers that recently you have
settled your accounts with us at six months, although
the practice in the trade is to do so at three months.

While we shall still be pleased to allow you a full six
months' credit, we feel bound to point out that no discount
can be given in future on such accounts.

Discount, however, will be allowed, as in the past, on
all invoices settled at three months.

Trusting that these arrangements will be agreeable to you and assuring you of our fullest attention to your orders,

Yours faithfully,
EXPRESS MOTOR ACCESSORIES, LTD.
A. G. Blackstock.

Letter Disputing the Deduction of a Cash Discount

Messrs. Maybrick, Ltd.

Dear Sirs,

We have to thank you for your cheque of £48.75 received this morning : but regret that we cannot accept it in full settlement of the sum of £50.

It is true that we allow a discount of 2½% for prompt cash : but this account has run for six months.

The account now stands as follows :

Per Invoice of March 12th,   £50.00
Received per cheque .   . £48.75
Balance outstanding .   . £1.25

We shall be glad to have a cheque for this amount at your convenience.

Yours faithfully,
Radio Spares, Ltd.

Letter Complaining of an Overcharge in an Invoice

168, Avenue Road,
Highford, Bucks.
Jan. 8th, 19—.

Messrs. Paul Jones & Co., Ltd.

Dear Sirs,

I am in receipt of your invoice dated Jan. 1st. As you will notice, the second item is for —— goods at a cost of £1.25. These were sent with the original order, but were returned by me because ——

I am returning your invoice and, when it has been amended, I shall be pleased to forward you my cheque

Yours faithfully,

R. Simpson.

Letter Asking for an Estimate

Messrs. Alldays & Brown, Ltd.

Dear Sirs,

We are desirous of having certain repairs done to the above premises. Roughly speaking, the work consists of

(1) ....

(2) ....

(3) ....

As the work is of some importance, we are asking three firms to estimate for it. Would you care for your Company to be one of them ?

We shall be glad to give a representative of yours an opportunity of looking over the premises any day next week (except Saturday), between 10 a.m. and 5 p.m.

Yours faithfully,

Derwent Morgan & Co., Ltd.

Letter Accompanying an Estimate

68, Globe Villas,

Wallerton,

Salisbury.

G. Smithers Esq.   April 11th, 19—.

Dear Sir,

A few days ago you were good enough to ask me to give you an estimate for certain repairs.

I have carefully checked over the work and now have pleasure in submitting the estimate. I may add that the figure quoted is for best materials and workmanship.

Hoping that my quotation will prove acceptable,

Yours faithfully,

N. Fitzwilliam.

Letter Informing a Company of the Loss of a Dividend Warrant

54, Amberley Rd.,
Appleton, Essex.
Jan. 31st, 19—

The Secretary,
The Premier Tailors, Ltd.

Dear Sir,

Early in the month, you sent me a dividend warrant for £20, in respect of 200 shares which I hold in your Company.

Unfortunately the warrant has been destroyed or mislaid. In the circumstances, would you inform me whether it is possible to issue a duplicate or, if this cannot be done, what course you adopt in such cases.

Yours faithfully,
K. Brightwell.

Letter to a Bank Manager Asking him to Stop Payment of a Cheque

51, Church Street,
Royburn.
July 8th, 19—.

E. R. Cox Esq.,
London & District Bank.

Dear Sir,

Will you please stop the payment of cheque 4248/6 dated July 6th. It was signed by me in favour of E. Palfrey Esq., the sum being £50.

Yours faithfully,
S. Dennis.

(Of course a cheque must only be stopped when there is some very good reason for doing so, such as its loss by the recipient or fraud.)

Letter Asking for a Cheque to be Redated

7, The Treeway,
Portaton, Somerset.
July 8th, 19—

The Secretary,
Anglo-Australian Timbers, Ltd.

Dear Sir,

I am enclosing a cheque for £15 which you sent me a little over two months ago.   Unfortunately, it has been mislaid until now and my banker will not accept it, as it bears a note to the effect that it must be passed for payment within one month.

In the circumstances I should be very much obliged if you would help me to secure payment.

Yours faithfully,
A. Dutt.

Wording to Use on a Promissory Note

London, June 15th, 19—

£100

Stamp

Three months after date, I promise to pay to F. R. Taylor Esq., or order, the sum of One Hundred Pounds sterling for value received.

John Heathcote.

Wording for a Joint Promissory Note

London, June 15th, 19

£400

Stamp

Six months after date, we promise to pay F. R. Taylor Esq., or order, the sum of Four Hundred Pounds sterling for value received.

James Fleming.
Arthur Alexander.

(Stamp duty must be paid on promissory notes. The duty varies according to the amount of money involved.)

Wording to Use on an I.O.U.

Birmingham, May 18th, 19—.

To Matthew Duncan Esq.

I.O.U. One Hundred Pounds.

£100

John Archer Smith.

(No stamp is required ; but if any additional wording is used to suggest a promise of paying, then the document has the effect of a promissory note and needs a stamp.)

Receipt for Money

34, Chelsea Walk,

Fulham,

S.W.6.

Received of R. Shipman Esq., the sum of ten pounds, fifty pence, in settlement of . . . .

B. Hicks,

£10.50.   April 3rd, 19—.

XI

BIRTHS AND BIRTHDAYS

Letter Announcing a Birth

56, Glendower Court,
S.W.24.

June 3rd, 19—

Dear Miss Fulford,

I am sending the following announcement to the Daily Telegraph " :

Hillman—On June 2nd, 19—, at 56, Glendower Court, S.W.24, to Mr. and Mrs. Geoffrey Hillman, a son (daughter).

I am sure you will be pleased to hear that Margery and the baby are both doing excellently.

Yours sincerely,
Geoffrey Hillman.

(On these occasions, it is difficult for a husband to write suitable letters acquainting people who are not altogether counted amongst the most intimate friends. A letter in the above form surmounts the difficulty in a neat manner.)

Letter in Reply to a Birth Announcement

64, Cedarwood Terrace,
Westbourne Grove,
W.2.

June 4th, 19—.

Dear Mr. Hillman,

I was delighted to learn from your letter that you and Margery have a son. You must both feel very proud.

Will you give my love to Margery and tell her I am so

glad she is doing excellently ?   I should love to come and
see her when I may.

It was extremely kind of you to let me know, especially
as you must have gone through an anxious time.

Yours sincerely,
Barbara Fulford.

A Letter of Congratulation on the Birth of a Child

Queensmere,
Avenue Road,
Kingston-on-Sea.
17—2—37.

My dear Mrs. Brown,

We were so pleased to hear of the safe arrival of your
little son (daughter) and trust most sincerely that you
are both making satisfactory progress.

How pleased and relieved you must be to feel that the
baby is a boy (girl) and that he (she) is strong and well.

I shall be so delighted to come and see you when you
are well enough, if I may.

Please accept our heartiest congratulations and every
good wish.

Yours sincerely,
Maud Crossways.

Letter of Congratulation to a Lady on the Birth of a Grandchild

Tessington Manor House,
Shropshire.
March 5th, 19—.

My dear Mrs. Gillingham-Lake,

Do accept my congratulations to you on the delight
of becoming a grandmother.   I was so pleased to hear that
dear Julia had started off with a son, and I am told that

he is a very bonny boy ! How proud you will be ! I am dying for the time to come when I may go and see Julia and her son. Have they decided on a name yet ? I am so glad to know that Julia has Mrs. Billing for a nurse. I believe she is excellent.

I hope you are quite fit, and that the family is in the best of health.

Yours sincerely,
Lily Holmes-Rogers.

Letter to a Relative Expressing Birthday Greetings

73, Marchmont Drive,
Cambuslang,
Glasgow.
February 18th, 19—

Dear Uncle Bob,

It is your birthday to-morrow, and I am scribbling a note to wish you joy and happiness on the occasion.

I am afraid I don't know much about the things that uncles like for presents, so, to be on the safe side, I am sending you some of the cigarettes you usually smoke. If these give you a half or a quarter as much pleasure as the train set did me—you know, the one you sent me on my birthday—then I shall be more than satisfied.

Give my love to Aunt Mary.

Your affectionate nephew,
David.

Letter Expressing Thanks for a Birthday Present

763, Archerhill Street,
Glasgow, W.3.
Feb. 20th, 19—.

Dear David,

It was very nice of you to remember my birthday, and still nicer to spend your pocket-money on buying me cigarettes. You will be amused to hear that there was not a single cigarette in the house when yours arrived, and I was wanting one badly. So they came at exactly the right moment.

Tell Mother that it is so long since she came to see us that we are beginning to wonder if she has forgotten us.

Why not bring her over next Sunday ?

All the best.

Uncle Bob.

Letter to a Relative Expressing Birthday Greetings

64, Brookville Rd.,

Birmingham.

January 17th, 19—.

My dear Aunt Elizabeth,

As to-morrow is the 18th, I am writing to wish you Many Happy Returns of the Day. Mother sends her love and best wishes at the same time.

I know you are not fond of receiving presents and hold the view that it is " more blessed to give than to receive " ; but in spite of that I am enclosing a little gift which I hope you will find useful.

Mother asks when you will be coming over to see us. Come whenever you can.

Yours with love,

Margery.

Letter Expressing Thanks for a Birthday Present

803, Coalville Rd.,

Edgbaston,

Birmingham.

January 19th, 19—

My dear Margery,

How sweet of you to think of me on my birthday. Your pretty and useful gift is very welcome, but what

I appreciate most are your thoughtful wishes.   It is nice of you to write and not forget me.

> Give my love to your mother.
> Your affectionate aunt,
> Elizabeth.

Letter Accompanying a Twenty-first Birthday Present

> The Limes,
> Kingswood Avenue,
> Chesterton,
> Surrey.
>
> March 31st, 19—.

Dear Vivienne,

I want to send you my congratulations on your Coming of Age, next Friday.   I hope it will be a very happy and memorable day for you.

Enclosed is a small gift which I trust you will like.

> Yours sincerely,
> Dorothy.

Letter of Thanks for a Twenty-first Birthday Present

> Queen's Drive,
> Chesterton,
> Surrey.
>
> April 3rd, 19—.

Dear Dorothy,

Thank you so much for the charming present.   It is really lovely.

I had such a good time yesterday that now I feel fit for very little.   Everybody was so good to me that I think it nearly turned my head.

When are you coming to see me again ?

> Yours sincerely,
> Vivienne.

XII

CIRCULAR ADVERTISING LETTERS

Here is a collection of letters suited to the needs of the shopkeeper and small trader. In most cases, the letter can be readily adapted for a business other than that mentioned.

Circular Letter Advertising Gramophone Records

Dear Sir,

We have a thousand different gramophone records here, and though we should not like you to have to listen to all of them, you would probably be interested in hearing a few.

Why not drop in one afternoon and let one of our assistants put on just the things you would enjoy hearing ? You can make your own selection.

Of course we shall be pleased to sell you any records you fancy; but we strongly object to your thinking that you must buy something just to please us.

If you don't hear any records you really like or really want, that's our funeral, not yours.

Don't trouble to make an appointment ı just come.

Yours faithfully,
RECORDS, LTD.

Circular Letter Advertising Radio Sets

Dear Sir,

Everybody knows which radio set is better than all the others. As a matter of fact, there are dozens that are as good as each other. The best set is the one you fancy most.

If you could spare half an hour and drop in here, you would be able to listen to a number of different sets, one after the other. That is the best way to find out which you like most.

If you would like to buy a set, we shall be delighted to sell it to you ; but it is not our business to try to make you buy something you don't want.

We take old sets in part exchange and we arrange for payments to be made out of income.

Yours faithfully,

THE UNIVERSAL WIRELESS TRADERS.

Circular Letter Advertising Radio Service

Dear Sir,

And then all was silent !

The wireless concert went on just the same, but he could not hear a note. The reason ? Why, there was something amiss with the radio.

If you do not wish to be blacked out when your favourite programme is on, we advise you to have your radio serviced regularly.

For a small fixed sum, payable monthly, we will see that your set is always in perfect condition.

May a representative call on you and explain our methods and charges ? You will not be under any obligation.

Yours faithfully,

THE ALBERTA ELECTRIC HOUSE.

Circular Letter Advertising Goods sent on Approval

Dear Sir,

This is the remarkable offer we are making to you !

We will gladly send you one of our celebrated Burnaby —— for ten days' examination. If, at the end of the time, you are not satisfied with it, you may return it without any question, and we pay the postage. If, however, you keep it, you send a P.O. for £5.

The Burnaby —— is such splendid value that we know you will not return it without some very good reason. That is why we are prepared to pay all the expenses of packing and postage.

Simply send the enclosed card to us NOW and the —— will come along by return. You will be glad you used the card.

Yours faithfully,
H. P. BURNABY, LTD.

Circular Letter Suited to the Needs of a Secondhand Car Dealer

Dear Sir,

If you want to be up-to-date, just jump into your car and drive along to our showrooms. One of our salesmen will tell you there and then how much we can allow you off the purchase price of a better car, taking your present one as part-exchange.

We have a large market for used cars, so can make you a really good offer for yours. More than likely, you will be surprised at what we are able to offer.

At all events, there is no harm in coming and seeing us on the matter. We can supply any modern make from stock or at a few hours' notice.

It would be a pleasure for our representative to call on you, if preferred.

Yours faithfully,
S. B. BROWN, LTD.

Circular Letter Advertising a Local Cinema

THE ROYALTY CINEMA
MARKET CROSS,
UXSHOTT.

May 18th, 19—.

Dear Sir,

There never was a more gripping film than THE BONES OF THE DEAD.   It is all about two brigands who shot at sight and then quarrelled with each other over a pretty, sad-eyed girl.   There are 401 thrills, 308 laughs, 16 mysteries and plenty of sobs in it.

It is showing at the Royalty all next week and we thought you would like to know about it.

The times are 3, 6 and 8.45, each day.

The seats are from £1 to £5.

Yours faithfully,
Roy Brotherwood
(Manager)   (*Stamped Signature.*)

Circular Letter Advertising Insurance

Dear Sir,

If your house were burnt down to-morrow, would you be ruined ?

If the gutter on your roof fell to the ground and injured a passer-by, would you have the money to compensate him ?

If an aeroplane crashed on to your house and wrecked it, would your bank-balance be able to stand the strain of the repairs ?

Many people sleep comfortably in their beds, in the belief that their policies cover them for everything. What a shock they might have, if one of these things happened !

You should talk these matters over with an expert who can explain to you exactly how you stand. May I come and help you in the matter ?   If you will send me a card, I will come at your convenience.   I have nothing to sell.

Yours faithfully,
H. P. J. Thornton.

A Circular Letter sent by a Shopkeeper Dealing in Equipment for Babies

Dear Baby,

There are lots of things you want, although you have only been here a few days.   We have all those things and, if only your Mother.or Nurse will call, we will gladly show them to her.

We are rather proud of our Perambulator Department, and don't forget that we have wool in every kind of shade for knitting all your winter wear.   We have hundreds of feeding bottles, thermometers and millions of safety-pins.

Get your people to bring you along and see the things for yourself.

With Best Wishes,
Barnes & Co., Ltd.

(The novel angle from which this letter is written makes it attractive and it holds the attention of the mother.   Consult the " births " columns of local and other newspapers for names where to send.   Write the envelope to " Baby So-and-so " and follow with the address.)

Circular Letter Relating to the Change of Proprietorship of a Retail Shop

Madam,

For a considerable time, you have been one of Mr. Alderson's most valued customers.   On Monday next, Mr. Alderson is transferring his business to me, and I am hoping that you will accord me the patronage with which you favoured him.

I have made myself acquainted with your special needs and can promise that your orders will be executed with precision and despatch.

Yours obediently,
B. A. Woodham.

(This letter should not be printed, but typed and individual names of customers should precede the word " Madam." The letter should be made to appear personal, as much as possible.)

Circular Letter from a Laundry

Dear Sir,

You don't feel your best with a strip of sandpaper folded round your neck. Yet some laundries we know turn out collars that are just as uncomfortable. They seem to take a delight in giving their collars a raw edge which is calculated to make the wearers miserable.

If you are a victim of collar discomfort, you have our sympathy and, what is more, we are prepared to make it practical sympathy.

Fill up the enclosed postcard and send it to us now—before you forget. At the same time, give instructions for three of your soiled collars to be put aside. Our van will call for them and, in less than a week, they will be returned to you looking like pieces of snow-white porcelain.

We shall be glad to perform this little service entirely free. If we can please you, and we know we can, that will be sufficient satisfaction.

May we ask you to fill up the card NOW.

Yours faithfully,
THE PERFECTA LAUNDRY.

Circular Letter by a Local Lending Library

Dear Madam,

The latest £5 Novel for 25p.

That is what we are offering you.

On our shelves, there are close on 20,000 novels, all of them either published this Autumn or quite recently. There are no old musty books that saw the light of day in Caxton's time and we have nothing to suit the maidens of the Victorian era.

There is no annual subscription and all you pay is 25p when you take out a book.

Our shelves are available from 9 a.m. till 6 p.m. The books are all within your reach and you can come in and make yourself quite comfortable while you are choosing.

Come along and take out a book for yourself, another for your husband and a third one for the family. In this way, you can all sit round the fireside during the evenings and enjoy yourselves.

Yours faithfully,
THE FICTION FURNISHERS.

Circular Letter Appealing for Funds

THE HOLY TRINITY AID SOCIETY
Longton, Durham.

December 17th, 19—.

Dear Sir,

How would you feel if you were starving to death? Yet, within a mile of here, there are more than a hundred families on the verge of starvation. It is a terrible thought.

Those of us who have to do with the Holy Trinity Aid Society know the blank horror with which these starving folk face each succeeding day. It is no fault of theirs that they have fallen so low. The fault is a social and an industrial one, far beyond their reach to remedy.

Can you sit in a comfortable armchair, beside a warm fire, and enjoy any peace of mind when you know that these poor wretches are deprived of everything in life worth having ? We think you cannot.

Will you send us a trifle ? Every penny received is used in providing relief. There are no salaries to pay and all workers are voluntary.

Yours faithfully,
Ellis Deigh.

Circular Letter from the Treasurer of a Hospital

THE JUBILEE COTTAGE HOSPITAL
Henderson,
Berkshire.

March 18th, 19—.

Dear Sir,

Twelve patients must be left to die or get better as best they can, since twelve beds in this Hospital have had to be closed through lack of funds.

At the moment, we have an overdraft at the Bank of £250, and last year we spent £150 more than we received.

Will you help us to straighten out our finances ? We are not in debt because we are extravagant : but because it is difficult to refuse help when help is needed.

We want to re-open those twelve beds as soon as ever we can. One Pound would come as a Godsend.

Yours faithfully,
A. Tucker,
Secretary.

Circular Letter for a Local Grocer, etc.

Dear Madam,

What would you think if somebody turned all your 50p pieces into pound notes? You would look upon him as a real good friend.

We will do more than that. We will make every pound you spend with us go as far as £2 spent elsewhere.

This is no idle statement. It is a fact which we hope you will allow us to prove. Our prices are the lowest in the neighbourhood and every non-proprietary article purchased from us saves you a few pence. Think how that mounts up in the course of a year ! And think of all the extra things you can buy with these savings !

We do not pretend to be charitable ; we are keen business people. We buy in the best markets ; we buy in huge quantities and we are satisfied with small profits.

Look in our windows and compare our prices. Our goods are unequalled for quality.

Yours faithfully,

S. A. BROOKS & CO.

GRAMMAR APPENDIX

In this section, certain matters of special interest to letter writers are given for purposes of reference

Punctuation

The chief punctuation marks are :

. The full stop.
, The comma (It is placed on the line)
; The semi-colon.
: The colon.
? The question mark.
! The exclamation mark.
' The apostrophe (It is placed above the line).
" . . . . . " The quotation marks (placed above the line).

THE FULL STOP is used at the end of a sentence or after a word that is abbreviated. Note that if any letter follows a full stop at the end of a sentence, it must be a capital letter. Also, see the note in regard to the Exclamation Mark.

Examples.—I went yesterday. Full stop at the end because the sentence is completed. *Mr. Jones.* Full stop after *Mr* because it is an abbreviation. (This is usual but not obligatory.)

THE COMMA has very many uses, but its chief work is to divide up sentences into small portions, so that the meaning may be easier to understand. But it is very easy to get into the habit of using so many commas that one is placed after almost every word. Therefore, observe the rule that a comma should be used only when necessary.

The value of a comma becomes evident in a sentence such as the following :

George King of England arrived in Paris. Without punctuation, the meaning of this sentence is ambiguous. Insert a comma after *King* and *England* thus—*George King, of England, arrived in Paris*—and the statement evidently refers to a gentleman who bears the name of George King.

Insert a comma after *George* and *England* thus—*George, King of England, arrived in Paris*—and the statement obviously refers to His Majesty.

Another use of the comma is when it replaces the word *and* or any similar conjunction, in order to avoid repetition, as : *The boy and the girl and the man went for a walk.* This is, of course, clumsy and the first *and* should be omitted. Its place is taken by a comma, thus : *The boy, the girl and the man went for a walk.*

Explanatory words or phrases, such as *however, nevertheless, in fact, consequently, therefore,* and *indeed,* when they come in a sentence, require a comma both before and after them, unless they form the opening or closing word of the passage, when they need only one comma. The following examples will explain this use :

She said, in fact, that she would come. (*In fact,* two commas.)

In fact, she said she would come. (*In fact,* a comma following.)

She said she would come, in fact. (*In fact,* a comma preceding.)

Regarding the use of commas where phrases are concerned, a sentence such as the following will make the rule clear. *The man gave the beggar sixpence.* Suppose we want to add to this sentence, the information that the man had a pocketful of silver, the wording becomes *The man, having a pocketful of silver, gave the beggar sixpence.* We have added a phrase to the original sentence and, because a piece has been added, it needs a comma both before and after it.

THE SEMI-COLON is used to separate two distinct passages which are put together to form one statement, thus : *Money is useful ; health is even more so*.   The pause, it will be seen, is more contrasting, more emphatic, than would be suggested by a comma.

A semi-colon is also used to mark a pause of some importance when a comma has been recently used to mark a pause of less importance, as : *My mind, you will perceive, is made up ; nothing you can say will alter it.*

THE COLON is no longer used much in ordinary prose.

It is still used, however, immediately before enumerating a list of things, as : *The following words are nouns : boy, cat, dog, fish, men.*   It may also be given immediately before a quotation, as : *The man said : " The time has come for us to return home."*

THE QUESTION MARK is needed at the end of a question, and here it is necessary to distinguish between the end of the question and the end of the sentence, if the two are not the same.   The following explains this matter :

(*a*) *Will you come to see me ?*

(*b*) *" Will you come to see me ? " she asked.*

(*c*) *" Will you come to see me," she asked ?*

(*a*) The first is merely a sentence which entirely forms the question and, therefore, no doubt can arise as to where the query is to come.

(*b*) The second is a question which does not comprise the whole of the statement.   Therefore, the query mark comes at the end of the question proper, and not at the end of the sentence.

(*c*) The third is incorrect because the query mark is placed at the end of the statement, and includes the question plus words that are not part of the question.

THE EXCLAMATION MARK follows an interjection word or an interjection phrase, as : *Alas ! the worst happened,* or

Long may he reign !   It is, also, commonly used to indicate emphasis or exaggeration ; sometimes even sarcasm, as ı *You are kind !* or *It is ridiculous !*

Note.—When an exclamation or question mark is used, it replaces some other stop, such as a full stop or comma. The two stops are not required. Thus, an exclamation or question mark and a full stop (or comma) are never placed side by side.

THE APOSTROPHE is used to show that one or more letters have been omitted.   It is, therefore, used in the case of possessive nouns, in order to show the omission of an old-time *e.*   *Examples.—The boy's book,* and *The B.B.C.'s policy.*

It is also used in such words as *don't* (for *do not*), *o'er* (for *over*), *'tis* (for *it is*), and so on.

In speaking of the letters of the alphabet, in the plural, or a repetition of numerals, the apostrophe is considered correct, as ı *h's* and *3's.*

QUOTATION MARKS, often called inverted commas, are used at the beginning and end of words, phrases or sentences which are actually uttered or quoted.   But note particularly that they must be the words actually used and not words very much like them.   For instance, *He said, " I do not think it will rain,"* is a repetition of the very words the person used ; therefore, the quotation marks are required.   But *He said that he did not think it would rain* does not repeat the actual words used, so the quotation marks are not required.

Note that quotation marks point towards the words that are quoted.   Thus, the opening marks curl to the right—like two commas upside down—and the closing marks curl to the left, like two commas the right way up.

THE DASH is used to mark a break in the continuity of the reasoning.   *Example.   He brought the money—not that I asked for it.*

THE HYPHEN, similar in form to the dash, though shorter, has an opposite function to perform. While the dash causes a break, the hyphen joins simple words in order to make them compound words. *Examples.*— *Ticket-of-leave*, *tug-of-war*, and *love-in-a-mist*.

When to Use Capital Letters

A capital letter should be used :

(1) At the beginning of every sentence.

(2) For the initial letter of every proper noun, such as a person's name, the name of a town, country, nation, etc.

(3) For the initial letter of every proper adjective ; that is to say, adjectives made from proper nouns. *Examples.*— The *English* people, the *Indian* mutiny, the *American* accent.

(4) Whenever the personal pronoun *I* is written, no matter where it is placed in a sentence. The vocative *O* is treated in exactly the same way ; but *oh* the interjection, is given a capital letter only when it comes at the beginning of a sentence.

(5) For the first letter of the words *Sunday*, *Monday*, *Tuesday*, etc., *January*, *February*, *March*, etc., *Easter*, *Whitsun*, *Christmas*, etc.

(6) For the first letter of every line of poetry.

(7) For the first letter of the names of the Deity, as *God*, *Lord*, *Almighty*, etc., and often for the personal attributes of the Deity, or for pronouns used in place of the name, as *His*, *Who*, *Glory*, etc.

(8) For the first letter of a quotation put in inverted commas.

(9) For the first letter of a title, as *King* George, *War* of Independence, *Daily* Mail. It is also advisable to use a capital for each important word in the title of a book, a play, etc., as *It's Never too Late to Mend*. This is preferable to *It's never too late to mend*.

(10) For the first letter of common nouns when they are personified, as *Come, sweet Charity*.

Rules for Spelling

There are hundreds of rules regarding the spelling of words in the English language, and, were a complete list made of them, it is doubtful whether it would help the average person.   Probably the list would be more confusing than otherwise.   Therefore, only the chief rules are given here :

RULE 1.—When a word ends in *y* and has a consonant preceding the *y*, and it is desired to change the tense or add a syllable to the word, change the *y* into *i*, and add the syllable in question.

Example.—Carry becomes *carried*, not *carryed*.

Note (a)—This rule does not apply when the added syllable begins with *i*.

Example.—Carry becomes *carrying*.

Note (b)—Nor does it apply when the addition is the possessive *'s*.

Example.— Lorry becomes *Lorry's*.

Note (c)—Care must be taken to note that this rule only holds when the *y* is preceded by a consonant.   If a vowel comes immediately before the *y*, there is usually no change. But there are certain exceptions, which are mostly words of one syllable.   The following , therefore, should be noted :

> *Pay* becomes *paid*.
> *Lay* becomes *laid*.
> *Say* becomes *said*.
> *Delay* becomes *delayed*.
> *Essay* becomes *essayed*.
> *Repay* becomes *repaid*.

Note (d)—The consonants are *b,c,d,f,g,h,j,k,l,m,n,p,q,r, s,t,v,w,x,y,z.*

The vowels are *a,e,i,o,u.*

Rule 2.—When it is desired to add a syllable commencing with a vowel to a word that ends with an unsounded *e*, omit the *e* and add the extra syllable. Thus :

Move becomes *movable*, not *moveable*.

Note (*a*)—If the word ends with *oe*, do not omit the *e*, but retain it and add the extra syllable. Thus :

Shoe becomes *shoeing*, not *shoing*.

Note (*b*)—If the word ends with *ce* or *ge*, do not omit the *e* when *ous* or *able* are to be added. Thus :

Notice becomes *noticeable*.
Peace becomes *peaceable*.
Courage becomes *courageous*.

Note (*c*)—If, by omitting the *e*, the meaning of the word may be obscured, the *e* should be retained. Thus :

Singe becomes *singeing* and not *singing*, as this would confuse with *singing* (vocal).

Note (*d*)—If a word ends with *ee* and the syllable that it is desired to add commences with an *e*, one of the three *e*'s must disappear. Thus :

Agree becomes *agreed*, not *agreeed*.

Note (*e*)—If the word ends in an *e* preceded by a soft *c*, the *e* is changed into *i*. Thus :

Space becomes *spacious*.

Rule 3.—The previous rule applies only when the added syllable commences with a vowel. If, however, the added syllable commences with a consonant, the final is retained. Thus :

Peace becomes *peaceful*, not *peacful*.

There are certain exceptions, however. Thus :

Awe becomes *awful*.
Argue becomes *argument*.
Due becomes *duly*.
True becomes *truly*.
Whole becomes *wholly*.

Rule 4.—No final consonant is doubled, except *f*, *l*, and *s*.

Note.—The following are exceptions to this rule : *add*, *burr*, *butt*, *buzz*, *ebb*, *egg*, *err*, *inn*, *odd*, *purr*, *rudd*.

Rule 5.—A one-syllable word ending in *f*, *l* or *s*, which is preceded by a vowel, doubles the last consonant. Thus : *ball*, *cuff*, *puss*.

Note.—There are a good many exceptions to this rule, as *if*, *of*, *as*, *gas*, *his*, etc.

Rule 6.—Words of more than one syllable ending in *f*, *l* and *s* :
  (*a*) Double the final *f*, as *distaff*.
  (*b*) Usually double the final *s*, as *harass*.
  (*c*) Do not double the final *l*, as *until*.
Exceptions are *atlas*, *alas*, *bias*, *Christmas*.

Rule 7.—*K* seldom comes at the end of a word of more than one syllable. For example, *critic*, *terrific*, *traffic*, but *trafficking*, and *mimic* becomes *mimicking*.

Note.—Exceptions are *attack*, *fetlock*, *forelock*, *paddock*, *ransack*.

Rule 8.—Words of one syllable ending in *k* usually have the *k* preceded by *c* after a single vowel, but have no *c* after a diphthong or consonant. Thus :
    Sack (short vowel).
    Book (diphthong).
    Bank (consonant).
Note.—Remember, however, *arc*, *disc*, *lac*, *zinc*.

Rule 9.—One-syllable words and words accented on the final syllable, which end with a single vowel and a consonant, double the last consonant when a suffix beginning with a vowel is added to them.

For example, if *ing* is to be added to the word *begin*.

which ends with a vowel and a consonant, the consonant *n* is doubled before the *ing* is added. Thus :

> *Beg* becomes *beggar*.
> *Begin* becomes *beginning*.
> *Glad* becomes *gladden*.
> *Confer* becomes *conferred*.
> *Rebel* becomes *rebellion*.

Note.—In the words *confer* and *conferred*, the emphasis is on the " fer " and, consequently, rule 9 holds good. But in making the word *preference* from *prefer*, the emphasis is thrown forward on the " pref." Rule 9 does not apply in this case, and that is why *preference* does not require a double *r*.

RULE 10.—A word ending with *ll* omits one *l* when a suffix beginning with a consonant is added to the word. Thus :

> *Skill* becomes *skilful*.
> *Thrall* becomes *thraldom*.

Note.—Exceptions are *illness*, *smallness*, *stillness*, while *dullness* and *dulness* are both considered correct.

RULE 11.—The letters *ei* follow *c*, but *ie* follow any other letter. Thus we write *receive*, but *believe*.

Note.—There are exceptions to this rule, but in almost every case the word itself gives a sufficient clue to the spelling. For instance, take *neighbour*. According to the rule, it should be *nieghbour*, but the sound tells us at once that this is out of the question.

The Plural of Nouns

RULE 1.—The general rule for forming the plural of a noun is to add an *s* to the singular. Thus

> *Cat* becomes *cats*.

RULE 2.—Nouns ending in *s*, *ss*, *sh*, a soft *ch*, *x* or *z*, form their plural by adding *es* to the singular. Thus

> *Gas* becomes *gases*.
> *Lass* becomes *lasses*.
> *Thrush* becomes *thrushes*.
> *Church* becomes *churches*.
> *Box* becomes *boxes*.
> *Chintz* becomes *chintzes*.

Note.—The above rule only applies to the ending *ch* when it is soft, as in *church*. If the *ch* is hard, as in *monarch*, Rule 1 applies and an *s* is added. Thus :

> *Monarch* becomes *monarchs*.

RULE 3.—Nouns ending in *f* or *fe* form their plurals by changing the *f* or *fe* into *ves*. Thus :

> *Loaf* becomes *loaves*.
> *Life* becomes *lives*.

Note, however, that there are many exceptions to this rule, and the following should be remembered :

> *Chief* becomes *chiefs*.
> *Dwarf* becomes *dwarfs*.
> *Fife* becomes *fifes*.
> *Grief* becomes *griefs*.
> *Gulf* becomes *gulfs*.
> *Hoof* can be either *hoofs* or *hooves*.
> *Proof* becomes *proofs*.
> *Reef* becomes *reefs*.
> *Scarf* can be either *scarfs* or *scarves*.
> *Staff* becomes *staffs* (a body of people).
> *Staff* becomes *staves* (a stick, prop, or musical term)
> *Strife* becomes *strifes*.

RULE 4.—Nouns ending in *y*, preceded by a consonant, change the *y* into *i* and add *es*. Thus :

> *Lady* becomes *ladies*.

Note.—If the *y* is preceded by a vowel, Rule 1 applies and an *s* is merely added.

RULE 5.—Nouns ending in *o*, preceded by a consonant. form their plurals by adding *es*. Thus :

Potato becomes *potatoes*.

Hero becomes *heroes*.

Negro becomes *negroes*.

But there are exceptions such as the following :

Octavo becomes *octavos*.

Piano becomes *pianos*.

Portico becomes *porticos*.

Proviso becomes *provisos*.

Tyro becomes *tyros*.

Note.—If the final *o* is preceded by a vowel, the plural is formed in the ordinary way, by adding *s*. Thus

Folio becomes *folios*.

RULE 6.—Some nouns have exceptional plurals, as *ox* becomes *oxen*, *mouse* becomes *mice*, and *child* becomes *children*.

RULE 7.—Compound nouns form their plurals by making the chief word into the plural. Thus :

Mouse-trap becomes *mouse-traps*.

Mother-in-law becomes *mothers-in-law*.

Opening doors to
the World of books

**Book Tokens
can be bought and
exchanged at most bookshops**